THE PASSIONATE FACT

THE PASSIONATE FACT

Storytelling in Natural History and Cultural Interpretation

Susan Strauss

Fulcrum Publishing
Golden, Colorado

In gratitude to some of my muses:
Doris and Robert Strauss, Trudy Sundberg, David Wyatt and
Linda Sussman

Library of Congress Cataloging-in-Publication Data
Strauss, Susan.
   The passionate fact : storytelling in natural history and cultural interpretation / Susan Strauss.
       p.   cm.
   Includes bibliographical references and index.
   ISBN 1-55591-925-1 (pbk.)
   1. Interpretation of cultural and natural resources. 2. Storytelling. I. Title.
GV181.18.S87   1996
306.4'8—dc20   96-6165
                                                CIP

Printed in the United States of America

0 9 8 7 6 5 4 3 2

Fulcrum Publishing
16100 Table Mountain Parkway, Suite 300
Golden, Colorado 80403
(800) 992-2908 • (303) 277-1623

Contents

Foreword

SAM H. HAM

SERIES EDITOR

All the world loves a story. But few of us loves, or can tell one, the way Susan Strauss does. Yet the most amazing thing about Susan—and that which separates her from most artists—is that she can explain to the amateur much of what she does, what is going through her head as she plans and orchestrates a story and what she is *intending* to do with her face, body and voice as she weaves a tale in front of a real audience. Hundreds of barely perceptible details come together at precise moments in the telling of a good story, and we forgive the master storytellers who are unable to summarize for us exactly what they were trying to do. Indeed, storytelling is complex business.

But Susan Strauss needs no forgiving. She, perhaps unlike any other storyteller I have known, is not only able but enthusiastically inclined to share her art with us. Her profession has been not just as a storyteller (as if that weren't enough), but as a mentor to others who want to compose and tell their own stories. Yes, her passion for stories, storytelling and storytellers will be clearly evident to the fortunate reader who turns these pages.

In *The Passionate Fact,* Susan envelops us with her own deep-seated love of the oral tradition. But be warned, she has an insidious agenda. Reading and re-reading drafts of her manuscript, I found myself each time succumbing to a sort of surreal dream state. Every wonderful story I had ever heard or told over the years came back to me in sometimes vivid detail as I turned the pages. I don't remember precisely when, but at some point I realized that Susan was doing this to me with a purpose. Her delightful descriptions, mastery of the metaphor and careful explanations of the "story" were themselves a story, one in which I was always the central character. She had me. I found each time I picked up the manuscript that I could not put it down. So compelling, so powerful were some of Susan's ideas that I sometimes phoned her impulsively to explore deeper meanings or to ask those "what about ... " questions we dream up whenever we are genuinely provoked to thought. In these frequent moments, I was far too excited to wait for her to receive my written comments in the mail. I had to talk to her *then*. I rather suspect some of you who are reading these words will smile when you realize that Susan has put you in a similar spell.

When Fulcrum Publishing asked me three years ago to edit a book series on environmental communication, one of the first volumes I envisioned was this one, and Susan Strauss was the *only* person I had in mind to write it. Having watched Susan tell stories and teach storytelling for so many years, there was no question in my mind that she would be the ideal author for this book. Widely acknowledged as one of the leading authorities on interpretive storytelling in the world, the only question was whether her busy schedule would allow her to do it. Fortunately for the series, and even more so for its readers, Susan accepted. The result is *The Passionate Fact,* in my opinion one of the most scholarly yet readable analyses of the art of storytelling produced in my lifetime. Readers new to Susan Strauss, as well as the many thousands of you who have observed her in action or participated in her workshops, will see in these pages a depth of understanding and insight into storytelling rarely brought to the printed page.

Sam H. Ham, Ph.D.
Department of Resource Recreation and Tourism
College of Forestry, Wildlife and Range Sciences
University of Idaho, Moscow

1

THE PASSIONATE FACT:
STORY SPEAKING VERSUS
INFORMATION GIVING

Some have dubbed the present and coming future the "Information Age." Television and computer screens have become the oracles for this important business of information giving. But in the midst of this proudly heralded most modern age, we must ask, what becomes of all this information? What information deserves our attention? How does this information affect our ability to live up to our higher potential for interaction in a respectful and socially responsible way with human beings and other life-forms with which we share the earth? What information moves us toward a deeper understanding of ourselves and the world, and what information distracts us from it? And why, in the midst of this most modern age of massive information processing, has the ancient art of storytelling enjoyed a renaissance? We might as well ask today as Henry David Thoreau asked over a hundred years ago when he discovered his neighbors' enthusiasm about a new telegraphing system that made it possible for Massachusetts to speak to Texas: "Yes," said Mr. Thoreau, "but does Massachusetts have anything to say to Texas?" Thoreau, Leopold, Muir and other great teachers of natural history have also been great storytellers, in the highest sense of the word. In explaining ordinary natural facts, they managed to touch something deep within the human soul. In this first chapter, we will look at how story speaking is distinct from information giving.

- How it demands introspection and self-reflection from the presenter to be effective.
- How it weaves together beauty and truth.
- How it creates relationship.
- How it translates content or information into image.

Among the traditional Karok, Natives of northern California, there is a special house built just for telling the old stories. A church or temple is also a special house just for telling the old stories. In the Karok story house the floor is the earth and in this earth floor is a hole. It is said that all of the old stories live in this hole. The storyteller sings to the hole to call the stories out. The stories may not come out, for stories are very shy. But if a story comes out, then the story-teller tells the story excitedly, holding it in the room and fearing at any moment that the story might slip away back into its hole. The stories are shy; they require a certain atmosphere of telling and listening to fully live in the world.

Among the Hassidic Jews, there is a story of a very wealthy man who hires a rabbi with an excellent reputation as a storyteller to come and tell stories at a celebration in his home. The rabbi travels many miles to the wealthy man's home, but when the time has come for him to tell stories, he can't remember a single one. All evening and the next day, too, he tries to recall even one story. Finally, the celebration is over and he leaves, feeling very embarrassed. Along the road as he is journeying home, he remembers one story. He returns to the wealthy man's home. As he tells the story, the wealthy man is shocked. At once, the wealthy man hears how much this story is also his own story; the story of how he decep-tively gained his wealth upon the misery of others. In the privacy of this audi-ence of one, the storyteller served the story and the story served its audience.

These two accounts imply that a story has a will of its own. This is a wisdom expressed by two different cultures. Their shared wisdom has evolved out of a participation with storytelling as a cultural, spiritual and artistic tradition ... a distinction that enables the story to be entertaining without becoming mere entertainment. The story is not something meant to be consumed as some aspi-rin, some antidote to life or some distraction from life. It *is* life, both in the classical messages it can convey and in the way it interacts with the teller and the audience to create meaning in the present. This is how the story has a will of its own. Nothing about it is predictable. Like rain, it is well received when it is needed, but not welcome when it is given without being wanted.

I met a modern-day Wasco man (Oregon Native) who, upon learning about my work, said to me, "We should hire you to teach our schoolteachers how to tell stories. I think it is a very new technique." "Well," I answered, "it is actually very old and it is not a technique." Whatever our cultural heritage, modern life has impacted our way of thinking about story, speaking and information. With the development of the industrial revolution and the age of computer-quick information came the notions that we can bend the world to our will and that things are meant to be of use. These notions, applied to storytelling, fall short of the art's true nature and service. They represent a materialistic way of relating to something that is not primarily of the material world. Certainly, one uses a hoe to dig the ground. Why not use a story to teach? Every great spiritual and politi-cal personality of history told stories. The difference is that when you use a hoe, the result is immediately evident and predicable. A story may take years of stewing in the listener's imagination before the listener says, "Aha!" and the teller has little control over what message a listener will derive from a story. With regard to stories, "will" is something that is generated out of both the storyteller's love for the world and ability to self-reflect rather than the desire to have a controlled result. It comes out of the teller's delight in beauty and truth rather than a need to instruct or entertain. This story "will" guides every so-called technique of the storyteller's art: the choice of words, quality of voice, body movement and even the choice of story.

INFORMATIONAL SPEECH

In our efforts to share our love of this particular beauty and truth we label as science or history, we need to ask: What distinguishes the workings of story from the giving of information? When I speak of story, I am thinking of a "way" in which content is expressed. This "story way" could find various forms such as personal anecdote, current event, history, folktale, legend, fable, parable, discourse of scientific fact, fairy tale or myth. Some of these forms are recognizable as story, yet some interpreters will object to including history or science on this list. History and science, they will insist, are information—by which they mean facts—even though the word "history" has the word "story" inside of it. Once I was asked by a colleague to participate in an interpretive training activity. She said, "Well, the first thing I'd like done is to have someone present all of the pertinent scientific information ... make sure we have our science straight ... and then have you give storytelling techniques." In this context, what did she mean by "scientific information" as something different from storytelling? Doesn't science tell a story? A story that is continually changing as new "facts" are uncovered and old ones discarded? When people use the word "information," do they mean giving the scientific story in a particular way that distinguishes it from the "story way" and therefore must be dry, lifeless or unrelated to a whole?

Let's begin by considering information as it is often characterized.

- A series of segmented items of content that are not necessarily related to each other.
- Content that is dominantly described by numbers, time measurement or otherwise quantifiable.
- Content that presents life as static.
- Definitions isolated from their context.

Perhaps more could be added to this list; hopefully, you have already begun to expand your thoughts about this question. Just what is information? In the modern world, we have become information junkies. We can listen to the news twenty-four hours a day. We have computers and fax machines that can produce and process information at high speed. The request for information even calls forth a special quality of voice from a speaker ... usually monotone and mono-rhythmic. Like our model news broadcaster, the information speaker feels that he or she must gather into their voice a particular tone that creates the impression of seriousness and that implies they know what they're talking about.

When we hear a great story told as information, be it scientific or religious, there are some dangerous, silent stepsisters that come along for the ride. They are the assumption sisters. They have us believing that information is fact and therefore truth ... the complete truth. These "information stepsisters" create an atmosphere that makes us feel in control of our world. "You've got the facts," they say, "and that's that!" Mystery and imagination are put on hold. Content given as information does not invite us to question or wonder. As if this weren't enough, they remind us constantly that beauty should not keep company with fact; facts are meant to be lifeless, serious and followed. Any great scientist, historian, scholar or religious teacher knows that truth is an unending journey of discovery, that imagination is the mother of great discoveries and that beauty is as much a part of science as it is of art.

By contrast, story does several things that information does not. Content expressed in a "story way" creates relationship, translates information into image and excites our imagining—our sense of wonder. The writer William Kittridge recalls the words of his creative writing teacher, Bernard Malamud: "Narratives would not be stories until some one thing changed, until the consequences of a moral stand were played out. There had to be a formal moment of recognition in which the world was seen in a new way. That was how stories worked and what stories were about ... learning to see freshly." (Kittredge, *Hole in the Sky*, 1992). This idea of seeing freshly is echoed in Freeman Tilden's idea that the interpreter's job is to provoke thought and again in Waldorf School founder Rudolf Steiner's idea that instilling a sense of wonder during the first eight years of a child's schooling was more important than any content. As we begin to investigate the function of relationship and image in story, we will see how they expand this sense of wonder. This is the opposite result of information giving, which can contract our world by shutting off the imagination and sense of wonder.

STORY SPEECH

Whereas informational speech compartmentalizes content, story speech creates a relationship between segmented parts and moves them toward a greater idea or new way of seeing. Within this synergistic flow, we feel ourselves taken into the experience of journey. In story speech, whether it is scientific, historic or mythic, the listener experiences the content as a journey. This is precisely what makes storytellers like Garrison Keillor so enjoyable. We know that he will give us the big point at the end, but we're not in a hurry because we're having so much fun with all the little points along the way. The journey toward the big point is full of surprises, and so our wonder is engaged. Coyote Stories and other myths create this same sense of journey with their fantastic series of dream experiences and general foolishness. Heroic stories, such as *Star Wars,* do this by presenting an awesome, seemingly impossible task for the heroes at the beginning of the saga. The heroes, whether an escaped slave in a history story or a research scientist in a scientific story, never know if they will succeed. We, the listener, believe at the beginning that the task is impossible. Yet, we are delighted by the hero's devotion to it. We know this righteous integrity. We may or may not have answered its call in our own lives. Still, to test our own choices with those of the hero, we have to find out what is going to happen. Our wonder is engaged. All of the content along the way, no matter how frustrating or obscure, is ultimately related to the outcome of the journey.

In addition, the message or the content of most stories speaks about relationship—or the lack of relationship—between the individual and aspects of the outer world. Upon a first reading of the Karok and Hassidic stories, we might say that they are about storytelling. After a second glance, however, we see that they are also about relationship. There is the relationship between the human being and the unpredictable ... between the spiritual man (the rabbi) and the materialistic man (the businessman) ... between the stories and the earth (the stories lived in a hole in the earth) ... between the creation of art (the storytelling) and timing. Even the act of sitting in the quiet space sculpted by the storytelling experience is creating relationship ... between the listener and the storyteller ... and between both and life. By the nature of story, we become engaged and thereby become the listener. There cannot be story without a listener. The listener may be moved by the story or judge it; be intrigued, angered or saddened by it. Still, once the listener is engaged, the story has created relationship. One of the primary aspects of storytelling, a way to distinguish it from activities that cannot be labeled as storytelling, is that it creates relationship. Even the simple stating of facts can be storytelling as long as the facts weave an experience of relationship and engage the listener in imagery. There is an old saying that a giant web, like a spider's web, connects everything in life. We humans tend to forget about it and act out of ignorance of it. Yet, when a true storyteller begins, it is as if the web has been tugged on and we feel its presence again.

Unlike information giving, storytelling can create a deeper relationship between the tellers and their unknown or forgotten selves—and, therefore, create relationship with a wider audience. Although you may choose to work with a story because you like the message of its content or "point," through the course of working with the story, you will discover much about it that you never recognized in the beginning. While you may be telling the story on a course toward a certain point or message, savor each moment along the way. A story told without a dogmatic attitude frees the listeners' imaginations to respond to whatever part of the story speaks to them most. Information spears the message. Story takes us on a journey around it and to it. For this reason, the tone of information is deadening. By contrast, the tone of storytelling invites us, seduces us into a world of imagination. When we hear "long, long ago" or its equivalent, our rational, information-bombarded mind says, "It's a story. Time to relax." In this willing suspension of disbelief, our intuitive mind is relaxed and enters into the realm of feeling. There it feels and intuits the "truths" of the story as they are presented through pictures, images and symbols.

Here we are again at that word, image. It is more likely that a listener will remember a specific image from your presentation than anything else. A good story shows what it wants to tell. Reciprocally, the messages of the classic myths and fairy tales can be told through their strongest images. Pick any familiar myth or fairy tale (for example, "Snow White"). Ask yourself and others what is the first picture that comes to mind from the story ("mirror, mirror upon the wall"). Then, ask others what they think the story is about, and you will see the relationship (jealousy and vanity result in self-destruction). Great "truths" are carried in the body of these pictures just as certain vitamins can only be carried in an oil base. If you want your audience to remember a particular idea, dress it in a strong image.

Natural facts are in themselves fantastic images. The tree of life. The apple. The rose. The maggot. These images are already telling a meaningful story and do not need to be dressed up. They dress up a world of myths and become the special imagery of fairy tales just by being so fully what they are. A rose is a flower like no other, and the dove can never play the hawk's part. Once, a colleague in one of my workshops was working on a story about bears. She wanted to leave her audience with two main ideas about bears in the national parks: One, bears aren't bad, they just have their own habits and priorities firmly established; and two, if you feed bears, they will learn to raid your camp, and if they raid your camp, they will probably end up being destroyed by Park Service staff. She translated these ideas into image by telling one bear's story through two points of view: a Park Service employee and the bear. Telling the story through the contrasting two points of view made her first idea clear. Since she had spent many long hours observing bears, she had a fantastic ability to take on the bear's mannerisms ever so subtly in her gaze and in hip and hand movements. In addition to the structuring of her story, the way she became the bear was absolutely engaging. At one moment in the story, the bear had come back to a camp where it remembered finding unlocked coolers the year before. Telling the story from the point of view of the bear, she said, "I raised up to get a better look at the things on the table. This human came running in front of my view and was waving his arms around and screaming. I looked to the side of him. The cooler was on the table." Here the teller becomes, actually *embodies,* the image of the bear's point of view. She created the park management point of view by juxtaposing the bear's telling with walkie-talkie conversations between park employees who refer to the bear by a tag number. Her second message is conveyed by juxtaposing the image of a bear as a number and as a personality or a living, thinking being.

Such a telling is testimony to the gift we humans can give to the world through our attentiveness. With our personal experiences, research and scientific observations of the world, we are constantly building a body of potential story material. Our skill as story makers is directly proportional to the degree of our attentiveness. If knowledge comes through direct experience and the average U.S. citizen watches twenty-six hours of television a week, imagine how limited their true knowledge is. When such an average person comes to your museum, park or nature center, you, who have spent those twenty some hours a week looking at bears or bugs or birds, can give them this lost experience and knowledge by telling your experience and knowledge as story. This is your culture, your inherited oral tradition as scientists and historians: to tell facts out of a passion for the world you are connected to—to build these facts you are most passionate about into experiences complete with senses, images, relationship and journey—in short, to make stories. After all, what is story but a field trip without the bag lunch.

Before exploring the specifics of how to do this (chapter 3), chapter 2 will give us a general familiarity with the different forms stories can take, which forms may be better suited to your purposes and how different story forms might work together to create a greater interpretive effect.

2

A WORLD LAYERED IN STORY:
TYPES OF STORY AND HOW THEY WORK

Once, when I was researching wolves for a performance of wolf myths, I visited a wolf refuge in Washington State. The staff biologist led me around to the various enclosures and as we walked and talked, he recounted his experiences with the various wolves. After listening to him for a while, I realized that his true-life stories were showing aspects of the wolf that I was finding in ancient wolf myths. I turned to him and said, "These are great stories. You should tell them to the public." He stepped back from me and shook his head. "Oh no!" he said. "I'm not a storyteller. I'm a biologist."

ANECDOTES

The first stories we learn to tell are the true experiences from our lives—anecdotes. These anecdotes are so close to us that we hardly recognize them as stories. Caught up in the immediacy of an experience, we often use tremendous storytelling skill without being aware of what we are doing. We might fall into character voice or gesture or take special care to set up the irony of the story we are about to unfold. But we don't think of ourselves as storytellers. It is said that the renowned painter and storyteller, Charlie Russell, slipped into one of his fabulous yarns only when casual company was around. The folks at the gathering would have a drink or two and then someone told a story, and Charlie had to top it. If someone stopped by to ask him to tell a story, however, he'd shy away.

This intimate venue of casual company is one of the best for the interpreter. Along the trail of a nature hike or passing a museum display, the story emerges from the interpreter like a touched-off memory; spontaneous, it catches the public off guard and they find themselves engaged in the experience of the interpreter before they even realize what is happening. Here again is the story's will in action. As in the Hassidic and Karok traditions described in the previous chapter, the spontaneous anecdote comes forth out of a calling or need instead of program scheduling, pedantry or routine.

The anecdote is the perfect story form for the confirmed "I'm not a story-teller" teller. In this venue of the anecdote told as an aside, the storytelling art seems almost conversational, but it isn't. Although an anecdote is casual in style, it has form. Chapter 3 will give a more detailed description of the forms an anecdote might take. For now, let us look at various anecdotes and their effects.

Point-Making Anecdotes

Once, at a conference, I noticed that the keynote arena was well stocked with spokespeople from various government agencies. Each followed the other with tedious reports of budget cuts and related bureau-speak. Within an hour, I had forgotten the content of these speeches with the exception of a story told by Gerry Coutant, who was the current director of visitor services for the Forest Service. I call this story "A Cricket in Washington, D.C." or "Gerry's Story," and it goes like this:

Gerry was walking down a sidewalk in Washington, D.C., with a Native American friend who worked at the Bureau of Indian Affairs. It was lunchtime in Washington. People were husslin' and busslin' along the sidewalks, and car honks and hurried engine noises filled the streets. In the middle of all this traffic, Gerry's friend stopped and said, "Hey, a cricket!"

"What?" said Gerry.

"Yeah, a cricket," said his friend. "Look here," and he pulled aside some of the bushes that separated the sidewalk from the government buildings. There in the shade was a cricket chirping away.

"Wow," said Gerry. "How did you hear that with all this noise and traffic?"

"Oh," said the Native man, "it was the way I was raised ... what I was taught to listen for. Here, I'll show you something."

The Native man reached into his pocket and pulled out a handful of coins ... nickels, quarters, dimes ... and dropped them on the sidewalk. Everyone who was rushing by stopped ... to listen.

Here is a shining example of the anecdote as the quick point maker. The anecdote drives home a point that establishes the theme of a speech, nature walk or interpretive talk. Presented at the onset of your interpretive program, such an anecdote can:

- Focus the attention of the audience, especially restless youngsters.
- Establish the direction of a program.
- Challenge a commonly held and inaccurate attitude of the general public.

"A Cricket in Washington, D.C." is one of my husband's favorite stories. As a state Fish and Wildlife Department biologist, he is asked to lead a few field trips every year for a local college wildlife biology course. He was often frustrated by the students' inability to remain quiet and attentive in the field. He began one such field trip with "A Cricket in Washington, D.C.," and the group's attention was focused on listening for the entire trip. Even the teacher mentioned the impressive impact of the story.

Contrary to the opinion of some, the true-life anecdotes of biologists are the foundation upon which facts are established. In addition to this, the public is often more inclined to regard a biologist's immediate experiences as "truth" over the same biologist's knowledge of research data. Remember that the average American watches about twenty-six hours of television a week. Living experience with the natural world is an increasingly rare commodity in a society that is more often bathed in virtual reality than actual reality.

The point-making anecdote is waiting to be formed from our everyday experiences. At least once a week my husband comes home with some story that clearly makes a point about people and wildlife. Such slices of life—like the time when the real estate broker called his office and wanted him to come out within an hour and kill a mother coyote and her pups before a prospective buyer came out to see the land, or the woman who bought property in winter deer range and wanted to know how to keep the deer from eating her tulips— are waiting to be shaped into the composition of story. One such story was used by a Yellowstone interpreter to address the danger of straying from the board- walks in thermal areas.

He told his audience a story about a friend who had led a group of visitors for a walk along this same boardwalk. His friend noticed that an elderly woman had strayed off the boardwalk and was sipping geyser water from a cup.

He came up to her and said, "Ma'am? Did you know that you're not supposed to drink this water?" She ignored him.

He straightened his hat and cleared his throat and said, "Ma'am? It is specifically against Park Service rules to drink this water." She ignored him still.

He bent down into her face and said, "Ma'am? If you drink this water, it's going to give you loose bowels."

She looked up at him and said, "Young man, that's just what I'm hoping for."

Consequently, with a bit of humor circulating in the crowd, the interpreter would find his audience better able to digest the dangers of straying from the boardwalk.

If you feel that your own life is irreversibly boring or if you just haven't developed your anecdote tracking skills, borrow an anecdote from a friend, relative, colleague or magazine. One of my all-time favorite anecdotes came from a *National Geographic* article on overcrowding in Yosemite National Park:

At age ninety-one, Carl Sharsmith still interprets at Yosemite every summer as he has since 1931. One summer a park visitor came up to Carl and said, "We just arrived here. We have only one hour to see the park before we have to get on the road. What should we see in the park if we just have an hour?"

Carl replied, "Well, Ma'am, I guess if I had one hour to spend in Yosemite, I would go sit down by that river and weep."

Connection with the World

Consider that an anecdote need not have a point to be useful in your interpretation. The point of a story can be to show a delightful or magical moment from life or to give an experience that moves the audience into connection with the world. An example of this is "Crow's Story" (Strauss, *Coyote Gets a Cadillac and Other Eye-Opening Earth Tales*, 1991):

Every spring in Portland, Oregon, like every spring in other towns around the world, baby birds are being born—and some of these baby birds fall out of their nest. People love to find baby birds and nurse them to health. But, if you find a baby, the first thing you should do is put it back in its mother's nest. Yes, in fact, the mother will take the baby back even after humans have touched it. If there is no other alternative, people in Portland, Oregon, will take a spring baby to the Portland Audubon Rehab Center.

It was to the rehab center that I went that spring, because it needed volunteers. When I arrived, they handed me a long tweezers and a tray of dry dog food that had been soaked in water. I was supposed to pinch one-sixteenth of a crumb of soggy dog food and feed it to each little bird in a cage. I opened the door to my first cage, and there were all those little babies with tiny little open beaks. I had to stuff one little soggy crumb of dog food after another into their mouths until a bulge appeared in the side of their necks—which meant they were full for the moment—and then on to the next cage. This was hard work!

When I opened the cage to the baby crows, I thought I was in heaven. Even though they were babies, those crows had big mouths. I wouldn't pick up one tiny crumb to feed them. I gathered four chunks of dog food and dropped them down their throats. "Gul-gul-gul-gul ... craw, craw, craw," and then they were ready for more. I became rather fond of the crows and began to learn their language as I watched them transform from what looked like misfit porcupines to dons in black satin cloaks.

About a month later, I was coming out of my house to wait on the front porch. Terry, my housemate, was getting ready to go into town with me. All of a sudden, a crow landed on the telephone pole next to the house. "Hey! Good morning, Crow!" I called up at him.

He looked at me and called, "Craw ... craw!"

I called back, "Craw ... craw!"

Well, this seemed to delight him; he called back to me, "Craw ... craw, craw!"

I answered back, "Craw ... craw, craw!"

Well, now he was all excited and shook up. He called, "Craw ... craw ... craw, craw!"

I answered, "Craw ... craw ... craw, craw!" At this moment, Terry was coming down the stairs, so, I said, "Hey, Crow, I have to go into town. I'll see you later."

He looked at me and said, "Craaaaawa," as if to say, "You do? Oh ... all right."

Now, that is a true story ... word for word.

This story makes several small points along the way:

1. mother birds will accept their young back after a human has touched them
2. mother birds work very hard
3. animals, like humans, communicate, but the main points are delight and relationship.

STORIES THAT MIGHT BE TRUE

As we make the transition from the realm of anecdotes to that of history, human and natural, we can pause in a realm we could call "stories that might be true." Once, when I was in Sweden, a man told me:

Some years ago, we had a terrible storm here in Sweden. A lot of starfish were washed up on the shore. Hundreds of them. I went out for a walk to look at the damage. There was a young boy running back and forth, carrying starfish back to the sea. I said to him, "Boy, can't you see how many there are here? It's useless what you do." He looked at me and said, "Yes, but to this one, it is important," and carried the starfish, still alive in his hands down to the sea.

Within the same two weeks of this trip, another Swede told me, "You know, we have a popular story here in Sweden ... ." He began telling me the same starfish story, but this time as if it had happened between two clearly fictional characters. I had been fully engaged by the first man's story and now thought he was clever to have clothed the story as if it was his own life experience. After the second telling, I wondered if the story had actually happened to someone. But whether it had or had not, the story held such a great truth and gave such inspiration that it might as well have happened.

Recently, my husband called a colleague in the Forest Service concerning trail construction through spotted owl habitat proposed by and for all-terrain vehicle and snowmobile users. The user group wanted to call it the Resort to Resort or R to R trail. My husband called it the Resource to Ruin trail. In a phone conversation, he called his colleague's attention to the specific habitat area and started to tell a story that might be true:

Imagine that you and your friends were going camping for the weekend up around the lake," he said.

"Yeah," she said.

"Well, you had just set up camp and changed into your sneakers ..."

"Yeah," she said.

"And the horizon was getting soft purple and pink streaks across the sky and a light breeze was moving through the leaves ..."

"Yeah," she said.

"And someone thought they heard a spotted owl ... ."

"Yeah," she said.

"And all of a sudden, you hear, 'Rrrrring-rang-rang-rang-rang-rrrrr'. It's a three-wheeler, and someone's going over the new proposed R to R trail!"

I heard this story from my husband's colleague as a testimony to the story's effectiveness. It was a story that hadn't happened yet, but it could be true.

"Stories that might be true" are just as valuable as stories that have happened, but they should not be confused with "stories that are not true." The fine difference between these two is apparent only to the tuned ear. One would not want to fall prey to stories crafted by propagandists such as Hitler's public relations director, Joseph Goebbels, who once said, "Tell the public a lie long enough and they will believe it." In general, "stories that might be true" can be recognized because they honor beauty, have the ability to create positive results out of adversity and inspire dignity and integrity rather than bigotry and narrow-mindedness.

ORAL HISTORIES

Returning to the anecdotes of Charlie Russell, we find stories that cannot quite be called historic fact because they were told under the influence of a particular teller's point of view and temptation to exaggerate. Yet, these kind of "stretched anecdotes," or "yarns," are valuable because they give an authentic flavor of a specific historic period. *Why Gone Those Times: Blackfoot Tales* (Schultz, 1974) is the so aptly titled collection of such anecdotes from the life of James Willard Schultz, a close friend of Charlie Russell. Such anecdotes can be called "oral histories," and they lead the way to the monolith of fact we call history. I will never forget a particular docent at Thomas Jefferson's home, Monticello, who delighted in telling stories about Jefferson's life that would, as she said, "never make it into the history books." Also, I will never forget listening to Cree story-teller, Ron Evans, as he tearfully recounted the acts of one of his tribe's greatest heroes. While the tragic story settled into a silence at the end of its telling, Ron said under his breath, "You won't find these stories in any history book. We keep these stories alive by word of mouth." I imagine whole unpublished histories of cultures kept alive in this way because the truth was too ugly for the dominant culture to record in history books. With these oral histories, cultures pass on lessons of life, values and aspirations as well as prejudices, fears and limited notions of potential. Both kinds of anecdotes, those that carry lies and hatred and those that carry the most unbelievable truth, serve history by showing an aspect of life not always articulated by major wars and legislative dates. It would be revealing, for instance, to present a prejudicial joke from the historic period of western Chinese labor camps in combination with statistics about death in those camps and legal cases related to early Chinese-American immigrants. A joke is often given in a "story that might be true" anecdote form.

Prejudicial jokes often create a belief that can be disproved by historic fact. Presented in juxtaposition to each other in a museum exhibit, both joke and historic fact can demonstrate the depth to which misconceptions can pervade a society. Jokes about Chinese workers in the western United States of the late 1800s made light of the value of a Chinese man's life. In this case, the joke mirrors a tragic history of murder and other civil rights abuses. The prejudicial joke (stories that are not true) presented along with documented history (stories that are true) give testimony to a degree of inhumanity and lawlessness in a society's history. Prejudicial attitudes also show themselves in dated history texts. Excerpts from these texts could be used in this same way, although jokes tend to be more poignant.

TRUE STORY: HISTORIES AND NATURAL HISTORIES

From anecdotes and oral histories, we find ourselves slipping into the realm of factual story or what we call history, natural history and the sciences. The ministers of this realm, scientists and historians, are often in great denial of their work as storytelling. The term "storytelling" seems demeaning and grossly insufficient for describing the tireless efforts of generations of scientists who ferreted out true facts about the functioning of the world. In reality, scientists and historians are observers and recorders of phenomena, from which they extract data, which in turn they synthesize into amazing and often very beautiful stories. Such professionals should feel that their work is no less important for being storytelling. If their stories are told with love, wisdom and a devotion to truth, they can inspire in their audience a lifelong interest in the subject.

To illustrate how easily the kingdoms of anecdote, history and myth can interface, I will recount my story of how I came to know the "Creation Myth of Yellowstone National Park." This story will also show how truth and the distortion of truth can dance together in the creation of history. Before we enter the story, I need to make a clarification of my definition of the term "myth," frequently misused in my opinion. A myth is not a false story, as used in the phrase "contrary to the commonly held myth ... ." A myth is truth told through an interaction of symbols, metaphors, motifs and archetypes. A myth is a true story that might never have happened, yet it reenacts itself in the lives of every human and in other living systems. Let's begin with the living system known as the U.S. National Park Service.

The first time I visited Yellowstone National Park was during a field trip that followed my first conference of interpreters. At the conference, I met a retired Park Service interpretive planner, named Don, who began his interpretive work in Yellowstone. When Don discovered that I had never been to Yellowstone, he said, "Come on! I've got a rental car. Let's go on before the others and I'll show you the sights."

We drove here and there as Don filled my mind with all the fantastic histories that anointed those beautiful landscapes. From the flight of the Nez Perce, to the mounds of the old cavalry posts, to the near-militant "takeover" by hippies in the late 1960s, Don was like a kid in a candy store—only the candy was stories.

Giggling sporadically between gaps in the running saga, he made a passionate last-minute decision to cross a lane of oncoming traffic to pull into a scenic lookout. "See this river," he said. "This is the Madison River!"

"Yeah?" I said.

"Well, this is where it all started!"

"Yeah?" I said.

"The Park Service! This is where the idea of the Park Service got its start!"

"Yeah?" I said.

"Well, in 1870 a group of explorers camped along this river near here and during an evening campfire, they decided that this was such a phenomenal place that it should be preserved for future generations to enjoy."

"Hmm," I said.

"Well, that was the idea of the Park Service! Imagine, even back then when everyone was thinking about how they could exploit the West. These guys had this visionary idea!"

The next day, Don and I were sitting together on the tour bus with the other conference attendees listening to a park interpreter over the loudspeaker when the bus approached the Madison River. "This is the Madison River," announced the young interpreter, "where the supposed story of the campfire took place and the idea of the Park Service supposedly originated. But this story can't be substantiated because only one of the men recorded this conversation in his journal."

"What?" Don was irate. "Who cares if it can't be substantiated! It's the Park Service's story. It's the Park Service's myth! The entire value system of the Park Service is contained in that myth! Every time a park interpreter starts the campfire before the evening talk, that fire is a reenactment—a symbol of that very first campfire. Does he realize what he's doing? He's destroying the Park Service's myth!" I nodded sympathetically as Don raved on.

One month later, I was on a plane bound for the National Conference of Interpreters, and I happened to sit next to an interpretive planner from the Denver office of the Park Service. I recounted this entire story with a decided tone of injustice. She answered me calmly, "Well, that story can't be substantiated. Nathaniel Langford was the only one in the Washburn, Langford and Doane party who recorded that this conversation took place. He went on to promote himself as the first superintendent of Yellowstone and proceeded to exploit the park as a hunting resort for the very wealthy of the day."

I sat in awe. There in the creation myth of the Park Service was the very controversy that plagues the Park Service to this day. Is the purpose of the parks to serve people through tourism or serve people and the environment through preservation?

Creating a Sense of Place

One of the hidden assets of "true stories" such as anecdotes, histories and natural histories is that they are a very subtle form of public relations. When a landscape becomes peopled by story, human beings begin to develop a sense of reverence for it. Stories give humans a sense of place or a sense of homeland. The hills and fields of Gettysburg would be just hills and fields were it not for the story that lives there. The same effect can be created by telling a landscape's geological story. Native peoples create this effect with histories and myths. I asked a Dutch friend for her initial impressions of the United States after she had been in the country for just three weeks. She answered, "The people here seem to be floating on the earth. But then, you all have only been here for about two hundred years, haven't you?" She comes from a culture of people who are not "floating," but are well rooted in their particular piece of earth since they have been peopling their landscapes with story for several thousand years. Chief Seattle speaks about the way people give their story to the landscape:

Every part of this soil is sacred in the estimation of my people. Every hillside, every valley, every plain and grove, has been hallowed by some sad or happy event in days long vanished. The very dust upon which you now stand responds more lovingly to their footsteps than to yours, because it is rich with the blood of our ancestors, and our bare feet are conscious of the sympathetic touch. Even the little children who lived here and rejoiced here for a brief season will love these somber solitudes, and at eventide they greet shadowy returning spirits. And when the last Red Man shall have perished, and the memory of my tribe shall have become a myth among the White Men, these shores will swarm with the invisible dead of my tribe, and when your children's children think themselves alone in the field, the store, the shop, upon the highway or in the silence of the pathless woods, they will not be alone. At night when the streets of your cities and villages are silent and you think them deserted, they will throng with the returning hosts that once filled and still love this beautiful land. The White Man will never be alone.

Let him be just and deal kindly with my people, for the dead are not powerless. Dead, did I say? There is no death, only a change of worlds. (*Aboriginal American Oratory*, n.d.)

Stories excite our imagining of a landscape or place. In 1979, I moved out West from Virginia to work for a traveling, outdoor school—a sort of academic version of Outward Bound called the High Country School. The administration, maintenance crew, kitchen and teaching staff consisted of three teachers and me. We were teachers of geology, history, natural history and language arts. When our bus, loaded with students, library and camping gear, barreled over the mountains into the deserts of eastern Oregon and Idaho, the staff would become suddenly ecstatic about landscapes, which to my Virginia eyes seemed barren and dull. What I came to learn was—when one has traveled days to sit at the shorelines of what was once a great prehistoric inland lake that helped the Spokane flood carve a good portion of the Northwest, or looked out to the horizon and imagined strangers coming into your homeland in trains of heavy wagons like a foreign army of tanks or pictured a time when there were so many salmon in the Columbia River, you could walk across the river on their backs— what I realized is that story is a gift that humans can give back to the earth.

More of What Natural Histories Can Do

Natural histories people the landscape, too, if we broaden our idea of the term "people." One can begin imagining how to tell natural fact as story, by imagining the various beings of the natural world as various "peoples." This concept first came into my experience through my work with Native American mythology and culture. It is a way of seeing the world that can be found among the indigenous cultures of many lands. One merely thinks of the various creatures as a separate tribe or people with a different culture, just as we think of the French being different from Americans, Arabs or Japanese. All are respected as sovereign peoples with their own particular lifestyles and language. Thus, the story begins:

Bottle Brush Squirrel Tail Grass People know how to survive in the desert. Well, they've lived here much longer than we have. So, you can figure that they've gotten their act together. You see, they live in one bunch so they can trap and hold water in their communal root system. They don't miss a drop of opportunity to conserve water. As Natives to the desert, water conservation runs deep in their traditional way of life. You can even see it in their dress. That fur on their leaves gathers and holds every drop.

... The Rock People are slow to move. They like to stay in one place. They have to be deeply moved to become energetic. If you ever strike a match from one, you should thank it for giving you the fire. You should always show your respect to the Rock People because they are the oldest people in this world. They were here before anyone else.

This way of speaking about nonhuman creatures does not anthropomorphize them. They are not living in brick houses like the Three Little Pigs. They retain their natural ways. Only our way of speaking about them has changed and, thereby, our way of seeing them has changed. As "a people," they are seen as unique beings with varied and fascinating ways of interacting with the world.

Just as our constructs of reality are broadened and enriched when we learn about the ways different cultures think about time, perform courtship, educate their children or care for their elders, so we will be broadened by learning about the various beings of our landscape. In human culture, a dead person may be referred to as a corpse; in the communities of Ancient Forest Peoples, a dead

Tree Person is a "nurse log." It has not left its community, but lives on into the next generation, which it feeds. Is it not equally true that elderly humans are rich with experience with which they can feed a younger generation? Is the judgment of an ancient forest as being "degenerative," because the trees grow slowly, an accurate description of an ecosystem that supports a rich variety of life or the projection of an impatient and impulsive culture that does not appreciate the virtues of age? The cultural point of view of the person telling the story can change the science. We must take time to reflect on how we are reading the book of nature. What wisdom might we lose in translation because of our human point of view?

When telling scientific fact as story, there is a great potential for revealing wisdom. It is precisely the beauty of this wisdom and beauty itself that fires the enthusiasm of the devoted scientist. Take, for instance, the story of Cyanobacteria, the Microbiotic People who live in the desert soils of the American West. It is their nature to be so agreeable and mutable that when they encounter a grain of desert sand, they meld with it. Actually, they chemically take a bit of the sand's body and mix it with their own. Because of this attribute, Cyanobacteria People actually hold the desert sand grains in slight and fragile suspension. Their great achievement is the creation of an organic crust on the desert floor, which allows air and water along with the seeds of all other desert plant people to permeate the soils. If it weren't for these quiet, mutable keepers of very little space, the deserts of the American West would be as lifeless as the Sahara. Is it not also true that we prevent our own lives from becoming a wasteland by making little spaces for the seeds of reflection and inspiration in the soil of our everyday life? Is this what the Cyanobacteria People are telling us? Or are they telling us about the heroics of the quiet, the fragile, the patient? Or are they telling us about getting along with neighbors? It depends on who is telling the story and who is listening. There are thousands of stories peopling the landscape.

LEGENDS

Legends, like folktales, fables and parables, are stories that might have happened, but became grossly exaggerated for the purpose of teaching or entertainment. Legends are usually pure entertainment. Interpreters may find them valuable for giving a sense of place, historic period or cultural point of view. For example, the tales of Paul Bunyan came out of an attitude of exploitation that accompanied the European-American opening of the American West. Native myths of the Northwest don't express this same exaggeration. The Paul Bunyan stories show us a landscape of grandeur and magnitude. Trees that took twenty men to encircle and rivers that roared like the Columbia needed a man as big as Paul with an ox as big as Babe to wrestle them into submission. These stories give us an expression of what the West once was and is no more. They also show a place where male brute strength could find unharnessed expression. This way of thinking about the wilds of America is currently under a tumultuous transition. In the Three Sisters Wilderness of Oregon, where on a clear day you might meet another hiker every fifteen minutes, I talked with a backcountry ranger. He described some campers who would make camp with their horses right next to an alpine stream and gather firewood by hacking away at a living tree. "These people think we're still living in the Wild West," he said. Paul Bunyan stories in conjunction with such a story and historic documentation of the changes in natural resources from the latter 1800s would make a rich interpretive program for that ranger.

FOLKTALES AND FABLES

Folktales and fables are stories that present specific, practical lessons on life. They seemed to have been created for learning about life with humans and are not often true to natural fact. Folktales and fables present a challenge to naturalists because they mostly portray animals as scapegoat parodies of humans. These animals are anthropomorphized. The Three Little Pigs build houses, the Big Bad Wolf eats humans, Br'er Rabbit butchers cows, Br'er Bear is always dumb and Br'er Snake is always devious. What's a self-respecting naturalist to do? Juxtapose! Juxtapose! Use the engaging quality of the folktale or fable to introduce the subject. Then, follow it with well-crafted true-life stories that reveal the authentic nature of the animal. Also, a folktale that incorrectly portrays animals could be coupled with a folktale from a culture, such as Native American, in which animals are mostly portrayed as they are in nature. For example, the bear is never presented as a stupid animal nor the wolf as a vicious or aggressive animal in Native American stories.

Before completely dismissing folktale characters, examine how they may have been developed. For instance, rabbits are not especially smart, but they are quick. Perhaps it is from natural rabbit temperament that Br'er Rabbit derived some of his trickster quickness. Also, snakes are not devious, but some can be dangerous. A common African-American tale, which has its equivalent among Aesop's fables, is the story of Br'er Opossum and Br'er Snake. In this story, Br'er Opossum is minding his own business walking down a trail in the morning light. He passes a pit that has been dug along the trail, but he doesn't look into it. Finally, out of curiosity, he looks into the pit and finds a snake there with a brick on his back. Snake pleads for help and Opossum pushes the brick off his back with a branch. Snake pleads for more help; he wants to get out of the cold pit. Reluctantly, Opossum lifts him out with the same branch. Then, Snake begs to be warmed by the comforts of Opossum's pocket. Opossum obliges. Once snake feels better, he comes out of Opossum's pocket and threatens to bite him. When an outraged Opossum recounts all that he did for Snake, Snake replies, "Well, you knew I was a snake when you put me in your pocket!"

Recalling the earlier discussion of "stories that might be true" versus "stories that might not be true," I tell this story with an attitude of dignity toward snakes. My desire is not to create fear of snakes nor to make snakes seem cuddly or forgiving. A snake is a snake. I introduce this story with a personal anecdote from my childhood in Florida. There, I would travel daily through a thick grassy swampland to my friend's house. My mother would always remind me, "Susan, before you go jumping over some rock or log across the trail, look on the other side. Snakes like to rest in the shady places. So, if you go jumping over that log and step on that snake, it's going to bite you. If it bites you, whose fault is it?" This is how, as a child, I came to respect snakes and learn about my responsibility to them. Children in my audiences today receive this same truth through the personal anecdote. The anecdote, like choosing the correct scarf to bring out a certain color in a coat, calls forth this meaning from the comedy of the Br'er Opossum story.

PARABLES

Parables are very short stories that present spiritual truths. The word "parable" comes from the Latin word, "para," which means "beside." The parable usually draws a comparison, by placing the listener's concerns beside those in the story. The parable is one of the oldest teaching tools and is common to the sacred texts of all religions. There is an old story from the Hassidic Jews:

> Once Parable met Truth walking along in a sullen manner. "Hey, how goes it, my friend? Why are you so glum?"
>
> "Oh," said Truth, "as hard as I try, no one will listen to me."
>
> "Here," said Parable, "try on my cloak. It is colorful and richly jeweled."
>
> Now, in Parable's clothes, Truth became very popular and everyone would listen to him.

Like the anecdote, a parable can help the interpreter make a quick point and focus the attention of the audience.

Just because parables present spiritual life does not mean that they have to be serious or have a heavy religious flavor. Some parables can be quite humorous, such as the stories of the wise man and fool, the Mulla Nazrudin (*Hoja da Nasrettn* in Turkish). His stories come from a mystical sect of Islam called Sufism and originated throughout the Middle East and the southern region of the former Soviet Union. Mulla means "master," as in spiritual master or wise man. However, the Mulla's stories give us a good laugh at the fine difference between wisdom and foolishness. Here is one such story:

One day, the Mulla Nazrudin was deeply engaged with the mysteries of God's wisdom as set forth in the laws of nature. "Here," he observed, "is a watermelon plant. So weak is this plant that it must crawl along the earth, and yet the Creator has given it the most heavy fruit to carry. And here is the mulberry tree with strong limbs carrying one of the smallest, lightest fruits. Where is the justice in this?"

The burden of this thought was so stunning for the Mulla that he decided to rest in the shade of the mulberry tree and contemplate it for a while. Suddenly, a breeze picked up and a mulberry fell ... splat! ... on his forehead. "Aha!" said the Mulla. "Now, I see. The wisdom of the creation is unending. Praise Allah that the mulberry tree does not carry watermelons."

MYTHS AND FAIRY TALES

The most difficult realm of story for interpreters and audiences alike is that of myth and fairy tale. Modern people hold many misconceptions about these stories. Mythic stories are seen as fantasy stories for a children's audience only or as the false beliefs of an undeveloped culture. How often have we heard the phrase, "We need to dispel that old myth ... " or "It's just a myth ... ." Myths and fairy tales are stories that speak their truth through symbols, metaphors and archetypes. Our own dreams speak in this same language. Like the parable, mythic stories are truth decorated in rich and mysterious robes. Myths are the sacred texts of ancient religions and initiation rituals. Fairy tales are derived from the same sources as myth, but they don't identify characters as gods and goddesses. Mythic stories are not stories created by a primitive minded people to explain natural phenomena before the advent of science. They are stories expressing the vast forces that lie behind these phenomena.

These forces and processes are often personified as gods or goddesses. Perhaps this personification occurs in most myths because these forces and processes are so vast and difficult to explain. For example, the gathering of forces that led to the big bang story/theory of the scientific community is spoken of in the Skidi Pawnee Creation Myth as "the Powers of the Four Directions and the Spirits Along the Skypath calling, singing and shaking their rattles." This personification is similar to what I described earlier in this chapter as "peopling the landscape" with scientific story. With regard to myth, however, the universe and its forces are "peopled" as well as the landscape. Again, I would caution the judgment of those who would label this as anthropomorphic. For example, Demeter, the Greek Earth Goddess, is not patterned after our mothers; she is the "Great Mother." She is Mother Nature—the big one, who nurtures life and takes life away. She is the birther and the swallower. She does not do laundry or bake cookies! She is occupied with baking basalt and hundred-year floods.

Because of their archetypal nature and because there are so many versions of each myth, they require great amounts of research to be told well. Myths and fairy tales have a great advantage for the interpreter, however. Even though modern audiences hold many misconceptions about them, they are stories that will fully engage the imagination. Taken to the place of their inner child, an audience will freely suspend their disbelief when they hear the words "long, long ago" and feel the essence of the story elements before they have time to think about them intellectually. Because of this quality, mythic stories can take an audience to its deepest appreciation for such archetypes as the tree, the bear, the wolf and mother earth, to mention but a few.

The subject of mythic story and its relationship to scientific story is so extensive that I have devoted the entire chapter 5 to it and part of chapter 6. For the purposes of this introduction, it is important to summarize the following:

- Mythic story and scientific story are not contradictions of each other. They are different languages for expressing some of the same truths.
- Science, or what we could call nature's story, is expressing an archetypal wisdom that is manifest in the world. We can learn from it. Much of it is still clothed in mystery, so the story is still changing.
- The outwardly manifested world of nature has a relationship to the inner human psyche. When we teach our child how to love the bear or the tree within themselves, they will be more interested in the bear or the tree outside of themselves.
- The archetypal and the biological are related.

Anecdote, history, the sciences, legend, folktale, fable, parable, fairy tale, myth and dream: These are the stories we are always making as human beings. Pick the sort that suits your style. As my father, a physicist and electrical engineer, once said, "I just don't get these myths. They're not my kind of story. I like history—I guess, because it's true."

3

LITERARY, VISUAL AND MUSICAL: STORYTELLING—A THREE-PART ART

In this chapter, we explore the specific ways in which "story speaking" works. Again, we will refer back to "information giving," as discussed in chapter 1, to distinguish the most subtle of changes that can shift your presentation of content into the more effective "story way" of communicating. Once you have found a story or body of facts about which you are passionate, this chapter will help you begin to refine your story with ideas about story structure, internal rhythms, image, metaphor, how sound makes imagery, word choice, tempo and voice.

> *"He, to whom Nature*
> *begins to reveal her open secret,*
> *will feel an irresistible yearning*
> *for her most worthy interpreter, Art."*
> —GOETHE (FROM SCHWENK, *SENSITIVE CHAOS: THE CREATION OF*
> *FLOWING FORMS IN WATER AND AIR,* 1965)

Essentially, interpreters of science and history must think of their work as art and their self as that of an artist. What is a true scientist other than a person in passionate pursuit of the mysteries of this great creation? Once uncovered, the perfection and complexities of the creation fill the scientist with a sense of beauty and reverence. The scientist is imbued with an even greater passion for discovery. What are true educators other than people who delight in watching the beauty they see in a subject ignite in the eyes of their students? What is our job as interpreters other than to serve the expression of this beauty and truth uncovered by a scientist or historian? What is a true artist other than a servant of beauty and truth? Equally as important as science or history in the training of an interpreter should be the study of the arts. This was obvious to Goethe and Tilden; why not for us?

If one looks closely at the storytelling art as practiced by various cultures throughout history, one will notice that all traditions, to a more or less subtle degree, weave three art forms into one: the literary, visual and musical. Storytelling is precisely such a successful communication form, accessible to audiences of various learning styles, because of this combination of artistic expressions.

A Literary Art

Storytelling is considered a literary art (even though it is oral and not written) because it shapes a narrative to create meaning or addresses a problem, a question, an imbalance or a desire. The visual and musical aspects of storytelling should dance in harmony with the literary aspect and never upstage it. One can tell when the literary aspect has been upstaged. In such a case, we find ourselves more interested in the presence, gestures or use of voice of the teller rather than imaginatively engaging with the story. Whatever artifice a teller employs, it should never detract from an audience's imaginative engagement with the story. Robert Frost speaks about how a poem works in his essay, "The Figure a Poem Makes." We could imagine for a moment that he is speaking about storytelling and hear his words as equally true:

> It begins in delight and ends in wisdom. The figure is the same as for love. No one can really hold that the ecstasy should be static and stand still in one place. It begins in delight, it inclines to the impulse, it assumes direction with the first line laid down, it runs a course of lucky events, and ends in a clarification of life—not necessarily a great clarification, such as sects and cults are founded on, but in a momentary stay against confusion. It has denouement. It has an outcome that though unforeseen was predestined from the first image of the original mood ... . It is but a trick poem and no poem at all if the best of it was thought of first and saved for the last ... . No tears in the writer, no tears in the reader. No surprise for the writer, no surprise for the reader. For me the initial delight is in the surprise of remembering something I didn't know I knew. (Frost, *The Complete Poems of Robert Frost,* 1965)

Frost is clearly speaking about the way in which a piece of literature moves and engages the imagination. Here, he speaks about poetry, yet we could just as easily apply his words to story. In hearing his words about how a piece of literature works, we already detect his interest in structure with such phrases as "the figure a poem makes," "ends in wisdom," "a momentary stay against confusion" and "remembering something I didn't know I knew." Yet, notice also that he is speaking in musical terms with such phrases as, "No one can really hold that the ecstasy should be static and stand still in one place," and "It has denouement." Information has a "static" quality, but story, poetry and music send meaning through us with a sense of movement. Also, notice his attention to the visual in the phrase "an outcome that though unforeseen was predestined from the first image."

Story Structure

When we work with personal anecdotes as interpretive stories, we first have the experience—cherish the retelling of the experience (painful or beautiful)—and then recognize that we may have good interpretive story material in hand. At this point, we may or may not choose to craft the story, that is, reshape parts of the figure it makes, frame it or enhance some aspect of color or dialogue. Sometimes life gives us the perfect story, complete as an art piece, and sometimes we are called to work with the raw experience as a sculptor with a piece of wood—bringing out the fine grains and colors of the story. Either way, one must maintain one's initial sense of "delight" or "surprise" in the telling of the story. Although every story has a form or "figure," we see it only in retrospect. Again, in Frost's words:

> The impressions most useful to my purpose seem always those I was unaware of and so made no note of at the time when taken, and the conclusion is come to that like giants we are always hurling experience ahead of us to pave the future with against the day when we may want to strike a line of purpose across it for somewhere. The line will have the more charm for not being mechanically straight. We enjoy the straight crookedness of a good walking stick. Modern instruments of precision are being used to make things crooked as if by eye and hand in the old days ... I tell how there may be a better wildness of logic than of inconsequence. But the logic is backward, in retrospect, after the act. It must be more felt than seen ahead like prophecy. It must be a revelation, or a series of revelations, as much for the poet [storyteller] as for the reader. (Frost, *The Complete Poems of Robert Frost*, 1965)

Finding a story's figure is as relevant as dinosaur bones are to our image of what dinosaurs looked like. It's not everything, but a lot hangs on it. Like a Christmas tree, it is on the story figure that the ornaments of the visual and musical elements of story are arranged. The story figure of folktales, fairy tales and myths usually seem more obvious to us than those of personal anecdotes, histories and scientific stories. The structure of fictional stories can guide us to finding a structure for nonfictional stories. I will illustrate very specific models of these structures in chapter 6.

Initially, we can take note of a few universally similar aspects of story structures. Although each story will unfold in its own unique way, all stories have some expression of the following aspects.

Beginnings

Spoken stories usually articulate the challenge of the story within the first few statements or images of the story. There isn't a lot of time spent on descriptions of characters or settings as there can be in novels or written short stories. The challenge may be:

- A question ("Nazrudin wondered, 'Why is it that the mulberry tree is so strong and yet carries such a small fruit and the watermelon plant is so weak and yet must carry such a large and heavy fruit?'").
- A problem or imbalance ("The king became more ill with each passing day and so his three sons vowed to bring back the firebird").
- A character's yearning or desire ("But Rabbi Arie wanted more. He wanted to understand the language of the birds").
- A creation is undertaken ("The great creating one called the powers of the four directions—called the spirits along the sky path—called them all together in one creation council").
- A character just decides to go out on an adventure ("Jack decided to leave his mother and make his way in the world").

Middles

In the middle of spoken stories there can be:

- The development of a conflict or ordeal.
- A search.
- A transformation.
- A lesson learned or an initiation.
- A series of trials and errors.
- An expectation or anticipation built up in the listener.

Endings

Spoken stories usually give the listener as strong a sense of ending as they give beginnings. While the end may leave the listener with an open-ended question, paradox or, as in Native American stories, a sense that life goes on, the storyteller communicates a strong sense that this is how the story will end. No matter what the ending, it is essential that the sense of ending is clear. This means that the ending provides two important services: (1) It gives shape to the narrative, and (2) it does not drag listeners beyond their interest. Endings can:

- Restore a balance.
- Pronounce a punch line or realization.
- Create the feeling of a rug being pulled from under the listener.
- Bring about a reunion.
- Pose a question or paradox.
- Create a new beginning.

- Show a consequence or punishment.
- Show a victory or defeat.
- Create a reassurance of continuance (life goes on).
- Return to the same place having become a new person.

In this journey from beginning to end, we may notice that a pattern unfolds—in retrospect, as Frost says. Still, we can usually begin to detect a pattern in a science or history story by paying attention to the same kinds of things that create patterns in nonfictional stories. The following four questions can help reveal a pattern.

What Numbers Are Repeated Throughout the Story? In the story of Snow White, she is seven years old when her stepmother first notices her beauty and orders her killed. Snow White travels over seven hills and seven valleys until she comes to the home of the seven dwarfs. The prince travels with her casket for seven days, until one of his servants trips over a tree root, which jostles the apple piece out of her throat and she comes back to life. In the Old Testament, seven is the number of perfection and the world was made in seven days. Among several Native American tribes, seven signifies the completeness of the universe (the four directions, the spirit world above and below and the overall creating spirit). Seven tones make up the major musical scale. Our bodies are composed of completely new molecules every seven years. Numbers contribute to the literary meaning of a story. Like seven, other numbers carry a body of meaning universal to many cultures and also scientifically described systems. This numerology of mythic, scientific and historic stories is discussed further in chapter 5.

What Events or Images Repeat Themselves Throughout the Story? When Br'er Opossum helps Br'er Snake for the third time, against his better judgment (in the African-American folktale, "Br'er Opossum and Br'er Snake"), we anticipate that something is going to go wrong. In the Russian fairy tale "The Firebird," Young Ivan ignores the wolf's advice three times. Each time the wolf helps Young Ivan through the consequences of his ignorance, we begin to notice that the wolf is an animal with extraordinary intelligence and power. The number three, which has its own numerology described in chapter 5, is also the common joke-teller's rhythm. In the old English tale "The Hundredth Dove" (see chapter 4), the queen's disappearance at the story's end is connected to a servant's single-minded execution of the king's order. The king wants to have no fewer than one hundred doves served at their wedding feast, but the queen severely objects. The story's meaning is made through a clearly drawn connection between the dovelike appearance of the queen and her resemblance to the last or hundredth dove, which is nearly impossible to catch. Repetition of events or images builds anticipation for the story's climax and reinforces a message of the story. Stories can have an intricate weaving of repeated phrases, slices of dialogue or images. The more intricate the weaving, the more epic the story becomes in style.

What Contrasts Exist in the Story? Consciousness loves contrast. Through either the battle or dance between contrasting elements, a story's meaning is created. Any trickster or fool is a personification of contrast. By doing just the opposite of what is deemed correct, they either demonstrate the unwanted or miserable consequences of such action, or they create something new in the world. As will be discussed in further detail in chapter 5, creation myths from many cultures show the activity of creation as a product of contrasts. Look for contrasts everywhere—in the personalities of story characters and their garb, settings, time of day, change of voice, speaking rhythms and so on. Contrast is such a powerful quality; we will meet it again in the discussions of the musical and visual enhancements of the story structure.

Who Is Directing the Action of the Story? Who Is Receiving the Action of the Story? Do These Situations Change during the Course of the Story? In the Japanese folktale "Akiko and the Wolf's Eyelashes," Akiko's luck becomes more and more pitiful until she receives the gift of seeing from the wolf. Stories in which heroes or heroines begin to direct the action of the story after they have received a gift from a wild animal or place are common in many cultures. Histories are often interesting because of the enactment of will or the lack thereof. Much of the irony and tragedy in the Nez Perce flight history of 1885 is due to Chief Joseph's repeatedly expressed desire to not fight. And what about the natural history of the salmon? In its willful fight to go upriver to spawn, its body has already begun the biological process of decay. What a contrast between two wills!

Story Skeletons

After considering these questions, the storyteller/interpreter prepares a map or a skeleton of the story. Each story could have several possible maps, because various stories can be told from what seems at first to be a simple tale. The best way to begin your map is by arranging the order and relationship of what you believe are the strongest visual images in your story. While drawing a map to determine the order of important images, you may notice that the four questions we've discussed start to become more relevant. You may discover that you want to draw the images and scenes from the story, and if you drew a kind of connect the dots between these images, you would see the figure. A few ideas (but certainly not an exhaustive list) follow. Please avoid thinking of these structures as recipes for making a story. Stories can form various hybrid figures. If we try to make our stories fit into a recipe form, they may lose the delight and surprise that Frost wrote about.

The Scientific Discovery or Unending Question Story

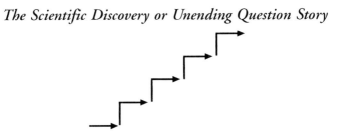

This is the story that starts with a question or an event, which results in another question or event, which, in turn, inspires another.

The Three Plateaus Story

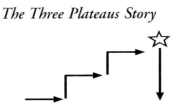

This story starts with a situation that builds or is aggravated through three events that increase the tension of the story. Then, a climax occurs and a resolution of the tension emerges.

The Spiral or Epic Three Plateaus Story

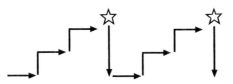

The spiral moves with the same pattern of tension and release as the three plateaus story, but it repeats this pattern to give the story's weaving a more sophisticated, complex or epic quality. Russian fairy tales and Hassidic mystical tales are both good examples of the spiral story. In "The Frog Princess" (Russian), there are two journeys. The first part of the story is devoted to the transformation of the princess from a frog into a woman. Although this first part makes a fine story (they could have lived happily ever after once she had completely changed), Ivan makes the mistake of burning her frog skin. She leaves him in anger and now his journey toward inner development begins. Perhaps the meaning in this long story and involved structure is that one member of a relationship cannot transform without also challenging the transformation of the other. The scientific stories of evolution and of ecosystem management have the same message and pattern. A storytelling scientist can put an audience in awe by revealing the intricate patterns of influence that exist in any one of several scientific processes or systems. Hassidic tales delight in the complexity of the universe often by telling a story within a story that has an impact on someone in the original story. Some of these stories are stories within a story within another story spanning over several generations of the story characters. In complexity, they come close to rivaling the story of geological time.

The A/B or Parallel Structure Story

$$A /\!\!/ B$$

Like many Japanese folktales, the A/B story first tells us a story about one character or set of circumstances. It then tells us a second story that on the surface appears to be about a similar character or set of circumstances, yet different results occur. This story structure shows very clearly how contrast within the form itself makes the story's point without any need for a moral to the story. In one such Japanese folktale, "Five Sparrows," an old woman heals a wounded sparrow and is rewarded with the magical appearance of wealth. Her actions come out of compassion for the bird. A neighboring old woman witnesses this fortune and intentionally hurts five sparrows, then heals them to gain the same fortune. Her reward is to be harassed by flies. The actions of both old women and the birds they work with are identical; only their intentions are different.

The Circle Story

The circle story gives us that sense of returning to the same place and seeing it for the first time. An example of this is the story of Rabbi Issac of Krakow who has a dream that if he goes to the neighboring city and looks under a bush, he will find a sack of gold. When he gets to the city and is searching under a bush, a passerby asks him what he is doing. When he tells his dream, the stranger laughs at him for being so foolish and tells him, "Why don't you go home and look under your own bush for a bag of gold." Embarrassed, the rabbi goes home to Krakow, sits in his yard and sulks then notices under a bush is a bag of gold.

The Triangle Story

The triangle story is a form that seems to suit many spiritual teaching tales, such as the Sufi Nazrudin tales. It sets up a situation and resolves it with a "pulling the rug out" sensation in a quick one-two rhythm much like a joke. In addition to "Nazrudin and the Mulberry Tree" (chapter 2), another example of such a story structure is the following Buddhist tale:

Two monks were making a long journey. Along the way they came upon a woman who couldn't find a way to cross a river. One monk came to her aid and carried her across the river even though a monk's spiritual discipline requires that he have no physical contact with women. The two monks parted with the woman after they had all crossed the river. Some miles down the road, the monk who had not helped the woman said to the other, "I can't believe that you broke your vow and carried that woman across the river." The other said, "I left her at the river quite a while ago. Why do you still carry her?"

As a Visual Art

There is an old adage about writing that also pertains to storytelling: Don't tell your audience what you want to tell them, show them what you want to tell them! Image is both the flesh and bone structure of the story animal. A reminder from chapter 1 is that storytelling translates information into image. The more detailed and specific the images, the more alive your creation will be. Image lifts us from the informational plane, where we feel "talked at," up to the visual plane, where we feel invited to become engaged and to enter the realm of experience, where we can make our own deductions. Notice the difference between the following two descriptions of the loon's call:

The loon has a beautiful, soft, joyful, reverberating call that can be heard echoing across the northern lakes of Minnesota.

From the creation myth of the Ojibwa:

After the seven Grandfathers had created the world, they gave every animal a voice—except one. The loon—what would they give to the loon? They were tired. And so, they decided to settle back for a while, rest and take a look at the creation as they had made it. When they finally settled and gazed over all that they had made, its beauty was so extraordinary that they each started to laugh with delight. This soft laughter of the seven Grandfathers echoed back and forth across the great lakes of the north country. It made such a beautiful sound that they couldn't help but laugh again and then decided to put this sound in the call of the loon.

If you were forced to give an interpretive presentation, to ad-lib, with no preparation except for your research, you should at least have an idea of the single strongest image enclosed in the subject about which you are going to speak. Then, you should send across your mind an imaginary slide show of five to seven images that mark important developments in this "story" you are about to tell. In a pressured, quick moment, making these choices will inform you of the story you truly want to tell.

We can gain a better understanding of the importance of image in storytelling and interpreting by looking at how our dreams speak to us. Nightly, they labor to communicate with us. Barely bothering with narrative, they scream at us in image. Pick any well-known story, "Cinderella," for instance, and poll your friends: What's the first picture that comes to mind from this story? You should get an overwhelming response for a singularly popular image—say, the glass slipper or the wicked stepsisters. Every story contains at least one powerful image that continues to radiate the relevance of the entire story long after it has been told. We can call these images the "power image" or "central archetype" of a story. In the Grimm fairy tale "Snow White and Rose Red," this image is the bear. Everything in the story builds to the entrance of the bear as a woeful creature seeking shelter from a winter storm, and then builds again to a second meeting with this bear as he is transformed back into a prince. The entire story is about roughness and civility or wildness and tameness. This character who is at once a prince (bewitched into the form of a bear by a dwarf) and a bear shows both tameness and brute force/civility and wildness. He is the image that carries the entire story's meaning. He is the central archetype of the story. He is a universal principal in the masculine nature of every boy or man. Over the years of telling this story, I have noticed that every boy in my audiences perks up when the bear arrives in the story. They recognize something of themselves in the bear. Once, after a public performance, a mother with her son came up to ask me if this story was on any of my tapes. I explained that it wasn't, but that I was considering putting it on my next tape. She seemed very impatient, and her son looked down and away in disappointment. She almost barked at me, "But my son HAS to have that story!"

We can learn a lot about storytelling, speaking and writing from studying the images from our dreams. Dream images are very specific. The image is not just a tree; it is an old gnarled tree or a thin one whose bark is cracking and pealing. They aren't just slippers, but glass slippers. I have observed two common problems that plague interpreters: (1) They want to give too much information and they cling to "informational speak," possibly out of some sense of security, and (2) because their knowledge or interest in the information is often superficial, their choices of images lack poignant details. Usually, someone who has had much life experience with a subject will move easily into rich, specific details when asked to speak about that subject. The first problem (overly informational) could be a natural reaction to the second problem. Therefore, when interpreters are assigned to interpret a subject they are not particularly interested in or know little about, their work should be to search out the finest, most specific details about the subject and use only the visually strongest three of these in their presentation.

Writer Ernest Hemingway was a master of invoking only a few, yet powerful, details. In his story "Big Two Hearted River," his protagonist goes on a fishing trip. Down by the river, he takes out a bottle that contains grasshoppers and gets one to come to the rim. Hemingway writes:

> Nick took him by the head and held him while he threaded the slim hook under his chin, down through his thorax and into the last segments of his abdomen. The grasshopper took hold of the hook with his front feet, spitting tobacco juice on it. Nick dropped him into the water. (Hemingway, *Collected Stories,* 1966)

Details such as "the grasshopper took hold of the hook with his front feet" and "spitting tobacco juice" create feeling, experience and meaning. Details like these are what have led people to believe that Nick is on this fishing trip to heal his emotional wounds from World War I. Whether or not this is true, these details give more than description or information.

The wolf is the central archetype of the fairy tale "Little Red Riding Hood." This image of the wolf as the devil is a false portrayal of the animal and was actually a projection generated by the leaders of the Roman Catholic Church to control heretics or critics of church corruption during the Dark Ages of Europe. Still, I decided not to contest the archetype but rather to play with its power in my own farce of the story, "Little Red Riding Boots Moves to L.A." My belief is that even though the original story is a biological lie, it creates an archetype of evil. Archetypes of evil are so attractive and engaging for human beings that it is useless to deny them (create a sweet wolf, for instance). Rather, I believe, it is best to surrender to the archetype for its engaging power and then to chip away at the real issues underlying evil, which are fear and misinformation—or the creation of fear through a manipulation of information. As in the original, my farce builds to the moment when Little Red meets the Big Bad Wolf. Because this moment is the wolf's entrance, and he is such a powerful archetype, he must be drawn with details that say something about our projections, fears and misinformation—and only three details should be used:

> There he was. Standing on his hind haunches—as if that was his natural stance. Bright gold chains hangin' down his hairy chest. Lookin' at her with those deep, bedroom eyes—the Big Bad Wolf—and he was a handsome devil, too!

Visual details have a special ability to cross-communicate all sense experiences (sounds, taste, touch and smell) through the power of metaphoric language (metaphors and similes). This is language that describes one experience by comparing it to another. Here are some examples from Robert Bly's descriptive poem, *The Hockey Poem.*

> *The goalie has gone out to mid-ice, and now he sails sadly back to his own box, slowly, he looks prehistoric with his rhinoceros legs ... .* Suddenly *they all come hurrying back, knees dipping like oil wells, they rush toward us wildly, fins waving, they are pike swimming toward us ... no, they are twelve hands practicing penmanship on the same piece of paper ... sometimes the players crash together, their hockey sticks raised like lobster claws ... .*
>
> *... but the men are all too clumsy, they can't keep track of the puck—no, it is the puck, the puck is too fast, it is too fast for human beings, it humiliates them constantly. They are all a little like country boys at a fair watching the con man—the puck always turns up under the wrong walnut shell. ...*
>
> (BLY, *WHAT HAVE I EVER LOST BY DYING? COLLECTED PROSE POEMS,* 1992)

Here, metaphoric language enhances the dimensions of what seems to be simply a sports game. With metaphoric language, the listener is hearing the crash of lobster claws, feeling the humiliation of country boys under the spell of a con man and feeling the pressure of twelve pens pressed to paper.

Finally, storytelling is a visual art because tellers must always see what they are speaking about. Out of this deep immersion into an imaginary seeing of the story comes the teller's feeling of the story's events and characters. In turn, out of this seeing/feeling comes the teller's vocal intonations, fresh choice of words and gesture. Without this fresh experience of seeing, the story becomes canned, too rehearsed and, in the worst sense of the word, the teller is "acting" instead of "being" the story. Despite all the fancy performance gimmicks or studied "storytelling techniques" a teller may conjure up, the audience will feel removed from the story if the teller is not seeing the story fresh in each telling. The story will not enter into their imagination or soul ... which is where the story should be. If it is not in the teller's imagination and soul, it will not enter the audience's. Here again is a distinction between "information speak" and storytelling. Information can be given without this seeing/feeling taxation on the speaker's imagination.

Seeing is creating. As you see the flight of the birds (as in this story), your eyes and gestures make just enough movement to create the experience.

Photos courtesy Jerome Hart

Photo courtesy Jerome Hart

In the heat of the imagination, a gesture transforms into a full character.

AS A MUSICAL ART

Storytelling fits into the family of literary arts, but technically, it is not literary. Literature actually means written. Storytelling is oral. Since it swims in the medium of sound, it is already musical. The driving rhythms, melodies and the tonal variations of instruments in rock 'n roll, rap and classical music create moods and images in the mind of the listener. Why should not the interpreter be trained in such a magical art as that of the musician?

In several cultural traditions, storytelling is intimately linked with music. Irish ballads are sung stories. Poetry was originally story set into a rhythm and rhyme so that the teller could remember lengthy sagas and speak them with such beauty and power as to hold the attention of listeners for hours. In describing a Navaho storyteller, folklorist Barry Tolkin refers to "the pretty languages of Yellow Man." These "pretty languages" of the storyteller are a way of speaking that can best be described as singing spoken word—singing the audience into a special place of mind in which they are connected deeply to the world. In many parts of the Islamic world, it is believed that one should always speak in a beautiful and poetic manner, for at any moment, one might die and the last words uttered from one's lips will go with you to Allah.

How often do we hear beautiful language spoken in our modern daily lives? Mostly, we are surrounded by the monotonous drum beat of "information speak" such as news speak, bureaucrat speak, doublespeak (Orwell's book *1984*) and so on. The sensitivity with which we should listen to others and to ourselves speaking is virtually extinct in modern society. One could blame this on electronic media, especially television, which is bent on filling the airwaves with speaking. Quality of speaking is not as important as filling time with noise. This phenomenon can be observed in many homes where the television is on almost all of the time and often ignored by people in the room. It is as if silence was something to be guarded against. Silence, as we will come to see, is essential to music, reflection and other processes of the imagination, gathering of certain scientific and historic data and good storytelling. For the moment, let's leave silence, the invisible partner, and explore the work of sound in these "pretty languages" of the singing speaker called storyteller.

To begin to practice this singing, we need to study its very elementary essence—the sounds we use to form words. In the average writing class, students might begin their exploration of language's sound by learning about such poetic techniques as alliteration and onomatopoeia. Alliteration is the gathering of words in a sequence that all begin with the same sound, such as "Lovely, lilting ladies loosing love lamenting." Onomatopoeia are words that sound like what they mean, such as "crash," "slam," "slap" or "buzz."

I have experienced an effect of sound that is even greater in its scope. To begin to understand this effect, one might ask two questions: When using alliteration, which sound should one choose to repeat? When choosing between two or three possible words that all mean the same thing, which one has more power because of its sound? In my farce "Little Red Riding Boots Moves to L.A.," there is a scene in which the Big Bad Wolf disguises himself as Grandma, jumps into her bed and prepares himself to meet Little Red. Up to this point in the story, the wolf has been frantically preparing his disguise before Little Red arrives. The tempo of the language is accordingly frantic:

> Then, the wolf went upstairs to Grandma's bedroom and found one of Grandma's finest, flowery, florescent nightgowns—with matching bonnet. He slipped on that nightgown and pulled the bonnet over his ears. Then, he jumped into Grandma's bed ... .

The alliterative phrase of the sound "f" ("finest, flowery, florescent") contributes to a frantic atmosphere, because "f" has a short, outward, panting, fluttery sound quality. To signal the tense moment when Little Red meets the Wolf, I slow the tempo by using the alliteration of the "k" sound:

Then he jumped into Grandma's bed and pulled the lace curtain across the canopy for camouflage—just then, the front door swung open—and—SLAM! "Grandma! It's Little Red! Come to bring you some goodies."

I chose to make this alliteration with a "k" sound because "k" is a choppy, cutting sound that affects the flow of language like pumping bicycle brakes on a fast ride downhill. Think of other words that contain the cutting "k" sound, such as cutting, contaminate, cataclysmic, contain and caught. They all communicate something of a sharp, clear or defining quality.

One could spend time with any sound and discover that it has particular energy that creates a special mood or effect. In this way, sound makes imagery. So, when we think of ourselves speaking, we might recognize that we are painting with sound. Onomatopoeia signifies words that sound like what they mean, such as pop or bang. But, let's go further with this idea of painting with sound. Take a word like stone or rock. Both of these words mean the same thing, but which one has smooth surfaces? You got a picture, didn't you? Stone has several sounds in it that create smooth surfaces. First there is the "s," which is a slippery sound. Then there is "o," which is fat, full, expansive and soft. Then there is "n," which is tentative. Rock is dominated by the "r" and "k" sounds. "R" has a growling, rolling, fiery quality, and "k" we already know. Although there is an "o" in rock, we do not hear it as "o," but as a tight, in-the-throat "ah." Because we have been educated in a literate culture, we have to be especially careful to pay attention to sounds that words make and not just their spelling. In English, the letters of a word are not always consistent with the sounds they represent. A listening audience is being swept into the sounds of language, not spelling. If you want to speak about rock in the context of some violent activity, you could reinforce or generate the feeling of violence by emphasizing the "r" and "k." Here are some other sounds and the connotations I feel they give. Try sounding them in some words and see if you agree. Try to hear, for yourself, the connotations of some sounds not mentioned here.

- T: a light tapping, almost like a match striking, that has a certain electric or spark quality.
- B: an expanding quality like a balloon, which then bursts at the end; a fat sound.
- D: heavy, as if the sound drops off the tongue like a drip in a faucet.
- A: an open, outward, relaxed sound. Expansive, as in a sigh (ah).
- J: a sound that slips out of the mouth under the tongue, like one slips for a moment on the ice and then catches oneself before the next step.
- M: a soothing, soft vibration between the lips; a warm sound.

- U: a slipping forth quality similar to the "j," but the "u" strikes forth like an arrow out of the slipping.
- TH: a soft, vibrational sound having an effect on the ear like the feeling of smoothing sand under one's hand.
- E: sharp, pointed, beginning in a slight hesitation and shooting forth in a piercing way (ee).

With this attention to sound, we may feel that we are dancing between the world of music (sound), visual art (painting) and literary art (meaning). This shows how intimately all three art forms are woven into the storyteller's art—how the parts of storytelling function like a healthy ecosystem.

Moving beyond the sounds of words, we need to become sensitive to rhythm and tempo. Every effective spoken presentation has an overall rhythm with changes in tempo. This can be thought of as a presentation's composition, just as a symphony has a composition. These rhythms, rising and falling, signal important points along the journey of the story or interpretive presentation.

Once I was at a public hearing for setting regulations on land use within a quarter-mile range of sensitive bird species that included golden eagle nesting sites. The room was filled with angry landowners who didn't want "some bird" regulating when they could run a chainsaw or build a new barn. Several government biologists testified about the phenomenal decline of these bird populations since the 1960s. They spoke about data and government mandates to protect species before they became eligible for the endangered species list. Nothing seemed to move these irate landowners from their conviction that they should be able to do whatever they wanted to do, whenever they wanted to do it, on their land.

Naturalist Jim Anderson spoke. He spoke in rhythms and pictures. "If there's an 'X' signifying a nest on your property map, I guess you can be angry with me because I'm the one who put it there. I've been studying the eagles of central Oregon for more than forty years, and I've seen how they're disappearing. What I'm trying to tell you is that you don't know how lucky you are to have a nest on your land. Those eagles out at Smith Rocks have been there for about thirty years ... and so have those eagles that nest over near your place, John. There used to be a nest out at Pine Mountain. It's gone. There used to be a nest out on the upper canyon. It's gone. Two men shot the adults. There used to be a nest out on ... ." By the time Jim was on his third "There used to be a nest," the pioneer-faced elderly lady in the second to the last row stopped making her snide comments and joined the stillness that was spreading across the room.

Jim's speaking was a perfect example of what I like to call "storytelling speak." There was no narrative line, but there was rhythm and detailed pictures. What was "some bird" all at once became a specific bird with a name for its home and a life story. The message of how the birds are disappearing was made stronger with the repetition of specific descriptions and the phrase "there used to be a nest" than it ever was with lists of numbers.

Rhythm is created through repetitions of patterns, alternations between narrator's and characters' voices or alternations between speaking and silence. There are rhythms within an individual sentence or phrase as in:

There used to be a nest out at Pine Mountain. It's gone.

Coyote was going up river. Then he heard it. That sound.

Well, I don't know Br'er Snake. You libel ta look me in da eyes. Then, ya gonna hypnotize me. Then, ya gonna bite me and lay me dead.

There is also rhythm created with the repeated use of a phrase. When phrases are repeated throughout a speaking presentation—or repeated with significant variations as in Martin Luther King's famous "I have a dream" speech, meaning can begin to establish itself much like the root system of a tree. Some people speak in this rhythmic way naturally. Some people find themselves speaking rhythmically only when they have become excited about an issue. Political speechwriters consciously choose these patterns. Often, I will consciously place patterns of language in a story to emphasize important imagery. Then, I make a map or musical score of the story in which each pattern builds on a previous pattern and thereby generates multiple facets of meaning—much as a symphony does.

Silence is an equal partner in this business of rhythm. However, novice storytellers and other public speakers are terribly afraid of silence. A confident storyteller knows the potency of a silent moment and does not fear it. The airy quality of silence gives weight to a statement just pronounced. It provides the "pregnant pause" in which a statement can ring for a while in the listener's imagination. ("I don't know," said Br'er Fox. [silence] "You might look me in the eyes." [silence] "Then, you gonna hypnotize me." [silence]) Also, silence grows heavy when it generates the anticipation of a statement or event. ("Then, the front door swung open" [silence] "and SLAM" [silence] "Grandma, it's Little Red ...") Silence can carry the true experience of time in a story. ("She would wait until he had fetched a good price for the coat and then she would have something good to eat." [silence] "She felt already better," [silence] "with some money from the coat and something to eat. [silence] It was getting cold outside." [silence] "He hadn't returned yet.") Silence is the petri dish out of which the life in the speaker's next words are germinated. It is in each moment of silence that the storyteller's imagination can hear itself, find the right image, find the right word—the right tone. Silence is the petri dish, the womb, out of which every story finds its first words—its first form.

While image and plot may be the meat and potatoes of the story, rhythm, silence and word choice are the spices—and character voice and dialogue are the salt. When working with any type of story, true or fictional, I look for key moments for a character to speak. That character could be Cynobacteria or Volcano as well as Coyote—and need not be anthropomorphized in order to speak. Character dialogue can have as much effect as poignant imagery or symbol; it shows what the story means to tell. Taking lessons from the fairy tales, notice that the only thing Snow White's evil stepmother says throughout the entire fairy tale are those famous words to the mirror and the flattering words to Snow White when she wants to sell her the poisonous laces, combs and apple. Everything she says has to do with vanity and deception.

In addition to the actual words, dialogue shows us the character through tone of voice. Tone of voice is the true guardian angel of the storyteller and the interpreter. Tone is distinct from volume and pitch. A voice can be loud or quiet (volume) or high or deep (pitch). Or, it can be high, loud and nasal-sounding like a whining dwarf character or high, loud and full like an opera singer. Tone is formed out of the resonance of the voice. As a generalization, I have noticed that often airline flight attendants speak out of a very skinny or nasal resonance that sounds like they are speaking through their noses or the top of their heads. This "head speak" is often produced by people who are in a hurry giving information that they are not passionate about. Speakers from the heart or deep body often work in experiential occupations, such as the country doctor, small farmer or veterinarian. Native Americans often have this deep body tone in their natural voice. People who are speaking out of compassion or love have it. Whether speaking as character or as narrator, tone of voice subtly shows the listener a hundred things. It may tell the character's weight, height or state of mood. It can create anticipation, tension and resolution. It can tell how you, the speaker, feel about the story or being in front of an audience. Tone of voice usually develops out of being fully immersed in your image of the character and then fully embodying the character in yourself.

A way to help yourself develop this embodiment is to imagine that your voice can resonate in different parts of your body. These areas are the nose or head, the heart, the stomach and the groin or tail bone. Some characters that might have a voice in these areas are:

- Nose/head: worried, nervous or complaining characters such as a dwarf or evil sorcerer.

- Heart: bold or arrogant, loving and warm characters such as the hero, the good queen or knight.
- Stomach: swallowing, big belly or heavy characters such as a monster, bear or giant.
- Groin/tail: big, fully empowered characters such as the earth, rock, god or goddess.

These are suggested images to help you playfully discover qualities of voice. Certainly, a monster could find an authentic voice that did not resonate from the stomach. Speaking from these various places as a narrator can either calm down or alert the attention of the audience. The voices do not need to be thought of only as character voices. Speaking in heart tones can calm or put an audience to sleep. Speaking from the nose or head can wake up an audience, shut down their listening or drive them out of the room.

Once, when I explained this work with voice to an interpreter in Sweden, he laughed and said, "Oh, yes. I can see how important this is for educators. But in my country, only actors, priests and politicians get this kind of training." This Swedish man's comment reminds us once again that as educators and interpreters of science and history, we deserve the same training advantages as those in other professions who hope to impact the thinking of their audiences. As artists/scientists/historians, we might think of our work as did the Persian poet, Rumi, when he wrote:

> *Today, like every other day*
> *we wake up empty and frightened.*
> *Don't open the door to the study and begin reading.*
> *Take down the dulcimer ...*
> *Let the beauty we love be what we do.*
> *There are hundreds of ways*
> *To kneel and kiss the ground.*
>
> (FROM MOYNE AND BARKS, *OPEN SECRET,* 1984)

4

Moralizing and the Message, or, the Moral to the Story and Other False Ideas about What a Story Does

There was a man who searched all of his life for Truth. After many years and much struggle, he found her. When she greeted him at her door, he was shocked to see that she was an ugly old hag. He stayed with her for some time. When he was ready to leave, he asked her what he should tell the world about her. She said, "Tell them ... I am a beautiful young woman."

From this parable we might conclude that the truth is ugly, but because we think it is beautiful, we will search for it. Or we might conclude that seeing the truth in its honest ugliness is a kind of beauty. How do the words of British Romantic poet John Keats fit into this discussion? As he wrote, "Beauty is truth, truth beauty— that is all ye know on earth, and all ye need to know." From this parable, Keats' poetry and Goethe's words, "He, to whom Nature begins to reveal her open secret, will feel an irresistible yearning for her most worthy interpreter, Art," we might conclude that beauty and truth have some kind of relationship.

Apprehension of these seemingly related creatures requires (as the story tells us) lifelong devotion and disciplined yearning. When one picks out a story to tell because one likes "the message," one must remember this is only the beginning of the journey toward the story's meaning and value. The "Truth" of the story will unfold in many messages—often unbeknownst at the beginning and only discovered through the process of telling.

A teller should always begin by choosing a story whose message seems good and important to the teller, but should remain fully open to the idea that a story can have many messages. In other words, the message you so loved at first in a story might be quite different after fifty or one hundred tellings. The various messages and shades of meaning a story has to offer will continue to reveal themselves to you for many years after you first began to work with a story. They will reveal themselves through your own associated life experiences and reactions from your audiences of various ages. As discussed in chapter 9, stories don't fully become themselves until they go through the fire of public reaction.

Such a birth by fire came to me while I was working on a series of performances of Hassidic tales (mystical stories from the Jewish tradition).

A Klezmer band had obtained a grant pertaining to mythology. They were awarded the grant because they had stated that a storyteller would tell Hassidic tales in concert with their music performances. I was to be their storyteller, but through the entire collaboration, the band leader continually tried to downplay the storytelling and build up the musical parts of the program. Because I had fallen so in love with the stories and the tradition, I fought to keep the stories in the program. By the end of our tour together, I was exhausted from the fight.

Our last performance was at the Jewish Community Center in Portland, Oregon. That night I was telling the story about the Baal Shem Tov (the founding mystic of the Hassidic Tradition) as a boy. In the story, the young Baal Shem Tov is orphaned. Upon his deathbed, the Baal Shem Tov's father tells his son that sometimes a challenge in life will appear like a great abyss over which it will seem impossible to jump ... and that sometimes all the greed and envy and fear in the world will fill people's hearts and they will be possessed by Satan. "At these times," he spoke, "you must remember that your soul is something that no one can destroy."

So, the orphaned boy was given the job to lead the village children off to school. Because he had learned the ways of nature, all of the children loved to go through the woods with him. Satan could not stand the joyful noise of the children, and so he possessed the body of a hermit. As a monster now, the hermit attacked the children and the young Baal Shem Tov confronted the monster. It is said that he reached into the monster and held his heart, which was black with all the fear and envy and greed of the world. The heart twitched like a fish out of water, but the Baal Shem Tov held onto it until it was quiet.

At this moment in my storytelling, a small child who had been sitting with her mother in the audience burst out in a blood-curdling scream. The mother carried the screaming child out of the auditorium. This was the straw that broke my back. I was tired of all the disturbances these stories had to endure during the tour. I dropped all my energy for telling the story and finished it out in a dead monotone.

After the performance, my dear friend and colleague, Linda Sussman, said to me, "You really blew it on that first story! Didn't you realize that all of the fear and envy and greed you were talking about was in the scream of that child? You had an opportunity to hold that heart, as the young Baal Shem Tov did. But no, you thought it was an interruption of your precious story."

Interpreters/educators often choose a story to tell because they idealize what they think is "the message" of the story. Often, a teller may feel righteous about "the message," but, in fact, have little or no authentic personal experience with this ideal. Such tellers may have a righteous tone in their style of telling or announce in some fashion that their stories will "save the world." Although most of us are interested in saving the world, such an attitude can generate a harmful separation from the public. The effect is: "We (the nature-loving, earth-saving, eco-muffins) are doing good by telling these stories and you (the less than holy) need to listen and learn." Native American Coyote tales provide a very wise and time-tested answer to this desire to teach without moralizing, although they are often misunderstood by the dominant culture (see chapter 7). I once met a teller who wanted to tell stories about all the good things ... world peace, honoring diversity, saving nature ... and she had been divorced four times. I try to keep my own righteous tendencies in line by remembering the words of a Pueblo friend of mine. He said, "People of the dominant culture are busy talking all the time. This talk keeps you distracted from facing yourself."

Enter innocently, with your desire to save the world, into relationship with the story. Once you begin to work with a story, its "ideal" begins to appear as a challenge in your personal experience and sometimes in the difficulties associated with audience reactions. If the ideal is truly a part of your disciplined spiritual yearning, then you will weather the storms of the story's growth and the ideal will transform into a richer wisdom based on your own authentic experience and soul-searching. In this tug-of-war process, the old hag, Truth, is nurtured. Only at this point do you have true power as a teacher and have something of true value to give the audience. Only at this point can one see how the hag's aged form bears fruit—the sweet fruit of wisdom. For those who have pursued Truth over time, she is both a very ugly and a very beautiful woman.

Here is a story:

Once ... I was in a rural California school giving a performance of my program, "The Bird's Tale." These are myths and fairy tales that focus on the bird as a symbol. As a preparation for the myths, I was trying to elicit qualities that the children in my audience would associate with bird life, such as freedom, grace or fragility. At one point, I asked, "When you see a bird soaring in the wind, how does it make you feel?"

A devilish look streamed into the eyes of a boy in the front row. He shouted out, "Like shooting it!"

I felt in that moment that he was judging me as some gentle nature lover he had learned to despise. He seemed to take special delight in the prospect of upsetting me with his comment. I was taken aback, but consciously did not show it. I said, "Hmm, yes, shoot it ... . Hmm ...

yes, kill it ... . Well, I suppose it's so beautiful up there flying around that you'd want to pull it down ... have it in your hand ... something that is so out of our reach."

I don't think the boy knew what to make of my response; he was somewhat stunned. I realized at that moment I would begin with the story I usually couch in the middle of the program because of its tragic weight. This was the perfect story for one who would kill a creature, alive and beautiful, as easily as opening a soda pop can—or at least he wanted someone to believe he would. So I told him "The Hundredth Dove."

This old English fairy tale is about a gentle fowler who is commissioned by the king to capture one hundred doves for the royal wedding feast. The king is marrying an extremely beautiful woman whose manner and appearance resemble a dove. When the fowler meets the prospective queen, he is so taken by her soft beauty that he trembles as he reaches to kiss her hand in respect.

The fowler is determined to be a good servant to the king and manages to capture a few doves each day in the meadow. But each day one white dove slips from his net. This doesn't disturb him until he discovers that this white dove is the last of the flock and the hundredth dove. Finally, he manages to grasp the dove as she slips from his net. He holds her in his hand and she speaks. She begs the fowler for her freedom in exchange for all sorts of treasures. None shake the fowler's profound sense of duty to the king. Then the dove offers the love of the queen. In a desperate confusion between duty and love, the fowler breaks the dove's neck.

The next day, he returns to the castle with the hundred doves, ninety-nine in a cage and the limp white one in his hand. He discovers that the wedding has been canceled because the queen has mysteriously disappeared. Knowing his part in this, the fowler gives up his service to the king and lives out his life in sorrowful solitude.

The brash boy in the front row sat with eyes as deep as a dove's throughout the telling of this story. In his eyes, I saw something of transformation. Who knows what might have been going on in his mind, but he sat in perfect stillness for the rest of the performance just as he had for "The Hundredth Dove."

Up until this experience, I had never given much depth of attention to the fowler character. For me, he had been a kind of decoy representing those who destroy nature through their simple-mindedness or devotion to duty above beauty. After this experience, I began to have compassion for him. I felt as if I had met his son. I started to see this character in myself—in those moments when too much devotion to "work" causes all the doves to disappear. The fowler transformed into one of the most interesting characters in the story because I realized how much he is contained in all of us. Instead of using the fowler to hammer home a moral in the story, I feel content to let the story end in mystery. After all, the story never states what is the relationship between the queen and the doves. Is she the hundredth dove or is she some kind of caretaker for them? What about her disappearance upon the death of the hundredth dove? Does she die or leave? And why? When I take my own moral advice and give up a sense of duty to produce a moral effect, the response of the audience is phenomenally alive. When I hold the mystery of the story in my heart, along with compassion for the fowler, the audience is on fire with the questions of the story. Children will often race up to me after a telling and ask: "Was the queen the dove?" "Where did the queen go?" "Why did she leave?" Morality is an internal awakening that may arise out of painful experience, a burning question or a yearning. From my experience with "The Hundredth Dove" and others, I believe a story that leaves an audience with burning questions actually involves the audience in the experience of morality and a proclamation of it.

PROCLAIMING A MORAL: AN IMPOSITION ON THE STORY'S FUNCTION

Most stories, and especially fairy tales and myths, can be butchered by people who think the point of the story is to give a single message. Inevitably, when I am traveling and happen to tell a stranger about my work, he or she will say, "Oh! Fairy tales and myths! I love them. They always have such a good moral." Myths and fairy tales don't proclaim a moral. They show things, such as images and consequences, but they don't moralize. If Zeus were still making new stories today, he probably would still be chasing virgins and cheating on Hera. And what about Persephone? Could she have ever become a goddess without being stolen from her mother and falling forever through the black nothingness of the underworld? What moral was she supposed to hold close? Don't mess around with gods of the underworld and stay mommy's girl forever?

Myths and fairy tales from world cultures show us images—images of transformation, death and rebirth, evolution, injustice, creativity in the face of adversity and choosing between loyalties, to name but a few. My experience with the California schoolboy and "The Hundredth Dove" illustrates a clue to the power of storytelling in the field of natural history education. Through the disarming context of the story—the listener thinks, "It's not really about me, but someone else"—and through the pictures created in the story, the teller takes the audience into a special world, which is, in fact, about the listener. It is a field trip ... with the experience of landscape, with vision of our place in that landscape and with a heartfelt, heart-endearing response ... but without bus or bag lunch. Actually, a storytelling experience is an internal field trip where the meadow is brought into the heart of the listener rather than the listener brought into the meadow—with hopes that the heart will follow. As the pictures seep into the imagination of the listener, the meadow becomes his or her meadow, his or her dove. So as the fowler breaks the dove's neck, the listener feels, inside, some of the fowler's remorse and confusion of values. There is no moralizing about the killing of beauty, only the experience. What seems to be the moral to the story is primarily useful for giving the audience a sense of closure. In fairy tales and myths, the story experiences and images are the vessels of message. It is a specific experience or image that the listener will find memorable, not the moral statement.

Within the great canvas of the mythic story are pictures that can reveal myriad meanings and fascinations for the audience's imagination. Once I was telling the myth of how Coyote freed the salmon into the Columbia River. In the course of the story, the greedy giant sisters who had kept all of the salmon to themselves were changed into two swallows by Coyote. The two flew up along the cliffs of the Columbia River Gorge and Coyote makes a pronouncement of a moral: "Soon the human beings will be coming. When they are fishing along the Columbia and they see those swallows, they will say, 'Hey, there are those two sisters who thought they could keep all of the salmon to themselves.'" At the moment that I gestured and described the sisters' transformation into swallows, a little girl in the front row followed the swallows' flight from my gesture up into an imaginary sky with her eyes and said out loud, "Oh! I wish I could become a swallow!" In that moment, she was in a state of beauty and not morality. Her response had nothing to do with the moral message that I dutifully announced to the audience as I marveled at her beautiful face. Had I been more present with her and less with my pedantic duty, I might have just stopped the story and with her said, "Yes!"

Although we can imagine what messages an audience might derive from our stories, and we can craft our stories toward a particular message objective, we don't always have control over what the audience will retain from the story in the end. Sometimes I imagine that, above all, the most important thing storytellers can do for their audiences in their effort to bring about some appreciation for environmental education and ethics is to merely create beauty and an authentic experience of the natural world. Whether it be in the realm of comedy, tragedy or eerie story, I think that when one creates an experience of beauty, depth and authenticity, one is bringing the audience into a mood of reverence. Out of reverence is born respect, and respect is the foundation stone of the environmental ethic. Think about how music can create an ethic even without any words, let alone a message. A piece of music can create images of landscapes and a sense of place that will bring tears to listeners' eyes and make their hearts swell up with love. Is this not as worthy a result as any moral objective? Ultimately, neither morality, beauty, authentic experience nor reverence should be objectives of the storyteller. Yet, they are all possible responses of an audience.

One of the most harmful things a storyteller can do to the effort of environmental education is tell stories in which the "moral" is obvious or easily anticipated or executed in a cutesy or "goody-goody" manner. This style often makes an audience feel "talked down to." The only place where this style of storytelling is permissible and sometimes effective is for children in kindergarten through second grade. In general, children of this age feel comforted by a clear sense of justice in which the bad guys are obvious and get punished. Still, you should guard against using a tone of voice that gives the impression you think the story is simple.

THE VITAL IMPORTANCE OF THE "BAD GUY," FOOL OR FALLEN ANGEL

The evil, bad or just simply wrong character holds enormous fascination with audiences of any age. They serve a very important role. Without great villains, there could be no great heroes. Taking a lesson from any great heroic epic, one never knows if the hero will succeed or fall into tragedy. The beginnings of heroic stories always convey the uncomfortable feeling of being completely overwhelmed by impossible odds. The eventual outcome is a serious mystery. As a species, human beings are much more interested in danger or in what might go wrong rather than what might go right. We often delight in mimicking evil characters. As Mark Twain said, "If nothing ever went wrong, there would be no stories." Because we are so imperfect ourselves, we are fascinated and sometimes delighted by imperfect characters and their struggles.

Enter, stage left, Coyote! Old Man Coyote, the creator, hero, trickster and fool of Native American mythology is a classic antihero and sacred clown—and, therefore, master teacher. The first time I met Coyote, I was researching Native American myths for a class I was teaching in a traveling outdoor school. Coyote was making his tracks, tracks, tracks through a Nez Perce story in which he meets up with a farting rabbit. Coyote falls in love with this new sound of farting and demands that the rabbit give him the means to produce "this thing" (the sound). After some attempts to dissuade Coyote's desire, the rabbit gives him his bow and arrows. Upon shooting the arrows, Coyote can produce farts. He goes off farting into the woods, delighted with his new toy. Later, we find Coyote barely able to walk. His anus has become too sore from all his farting. Finally, after some trickery and threats, he discovers that the way to get rid of "this thing" is to "leave the bow and arrows alone."

Here is the perfect story for anyone overly possessed by desire, materialism or greed. Farting is the perfect analogy for that "thing" we must have. Avarice, like farting, comes natural to human beings; it is loud, smelly and out of our control, and we laugh about it. Everything taboo and anything we might secretly imagine doing, Coyote does. This is the beauty of the Coyote Stories. Coyote displays a story behavior the audience can experience and through him enjoy what they might not otherwise want to admit doing. As Sigmund Freud said, "Art serves as nothing else can to reconcile men to the personal sacrifices they must make to maintain their civilization." (from Ramsey, *Coyote Was Going There: Indian Literature of the Oregon Country,* 1977) Inevitably, when an auditorium full of children are finding their seats before a performance and a teacher is warning the boys in the back row that they'd better be quiet or they're "out," those are the first children to become completely focused on Coyote when he enters the imaginary playing field.

The morality of Coyote Stories is complex. Sometimes Coyote's foolishness can bring about good results, which goes to show that intention is not everything. Sometimes his foolishness can bring on painful consequences. Sometimes Coyote will get by completely with his ribaldry, which shows that you better not always count on justice. Sometimes Coyote exhibits foolish behavior in one part of the story and creative, risk-taking, heroic or generous behavior in another part. As a Navaho friend of mine once said, "Now I understand why my grandmother told me Coyote Stories. She was teaching me about balance—the potential for creating good and bad that lives in each of us—that we must see this potential in ourselves and hold it in balance for things to go well in the world."

In this chapter, I speak primarily about Coyote's negative aspects without fully addressing the bawdy aspect of the stories. In chapter 7, I will speak more fully about the positive aspects of Coyote and the complexity of this character. Out of respect for Coyote, the creator, Native elders have told me that they never laugh at Coyote, only at his behavior. To laugh at Coyote would be very disrespectful to the creator and, therefore, dangerous.

One of the great gifts of the Coyote Stories is that if they teach, it is not through moralizing, but through both positive and negative role modeling. Coyote is an attractive character because we anticipate that some humorous, clever or creative behavior will follow his nasty or foolish behavior. We feel engaged and not condemned or limited by his model adventures. He helps us to laugh at ourselves, which is the first step toward self-transformation. This is why he is known as the sacred fool. In the two stories, "Coyote and the Grass People" and "Monster Woman at the Coast" (from Strauss, *Coyote Stories for Children: Tales from Native America,* 1991), Coyote brags. In the first story, his bragging and overinflated ego cause him a lot of trouble. In the second story, they save the Animal People from a holocaust. One behavior can have different effects. We can see this again in the Flathead story of how Rattlesnake saves the people by putting its poison into the monster's stew. Even poison has its good uses.

Coyote Stories don't identify one behavior as bad and another as good. They show us situations in which the behavior gathers a consequence. Once while traveling, I was a guest in a couple's home. I noticed that whenever the wife left the house, the husband would make increasing references to his past extramarital affairs and his ideas about "open" relationships. Of course, I wondered why he thought I would be interested. At dinner one night, I brought up the subject of Coyote Stories and told a Karok story about the time Coyote went to the dances without his wife (see chapter 7). Coyote met someone at the dances after whom he lusted. But, when Coyote took her outside and began kissing her, she turned into his wife! Coyote threw her into the bushes and ran home. There he found his wife sleeping, so Coyote went back to the dances. In time, he met another woman who inspired a great lust in him. But, again, when Coyote took her outside to satisfy his desire, she changed into his wife. Coyote thought she was an evil spirit and beat her. Then, he ran home where he found his wife sleeping still. When Coyote returned to the dances, all of the women there looked like his wife. Following this telling, the husband never again mentioned extramarital affairs while I was a guest. I don't know if my story impacted this man's morality, but at least it altered his behavior while he was around me.

As my colleague, storyteller Michael Parent, said, "Storytelling is the most eloquent way that human beings can speak to one another." Storytelling is the most eloquent way because it moves with its dress of images and engaging mysteries in, out of and around morality. Like some fantastic dancing partner, story whirls us into the experience of morality. Inside story, we forget ourselves and dance with the story's questions, conflicts, complexities, consequences and positive and negative role models. There should be no question that story and storytelling are related to morality. After all, morality is the discussion of how behavior impacts others for better or worse—the source of all good stories, according to Mark Twain. Yet there should be many questions inspired by this chapter as to how one should work with our perceptions of these moralities. Some may be:

- How do you reflect on your own morality (truth/beauty) while working with a story and an audience's reactions to your telling of the story?
- How do you allow the audience to be free in their responses to the many messages of a story?
- How do you expand your understanding of a story and yourself through telling it without losing a sense of passion or conviction in telling it?
- How do you learn from the villains and fools in your stories?
- How do you enjoy and value other aspects of the story besides its "lessons" (the senses, landscapes, creatures—the "field trip" of a story)?

The ultimate objective of the storyteller should be to enter the story fully and to remain open to its mystery. Let it teach you; enjoy each facet of the story along the path of its unfolding. This is not to say that you should give up your interest in a particular message of the story. Rather, you should notice everything that goes on around your telling of the story in addition to the audience's reactions to "the message." I remember a story told to me by a Dutch colleague, Bram Vander Wurff. We were commiserating about how lonely we feel after a school storytelling assembly. We agreed that the moments inside the story world with the children created such an intimate feeling that leaving the school often felt like being ripped away. Bram told of one school where he had visited as a storyteller several times. On one such visit, a young boy walked up to him just before he was going to begin. Bram noticed a teacher, with a worried look, try to catch up with the boy and stop him. The boy said to Bram, "My father died yesterday in a car accident." "Oh," said Bram. "Are you able to cry about it yet?" "No," said the boy and he went to sit with the other children for the stories. Two things impressed me: (1) how Bram allowed the child to have his own feelings, and (2) how the child viewed Bram, the storyteller and virtual stranger, as a worthy ear for such personal news. Bram felt that because storytelling creates a place wherein we can speak about things we usually can't in mainstream life, the boy felt comfortable sharing something so intimate with him. It was as if Bram, the storyteller, was the keeper of a special place wherein we are allowed to be tender, reflective or vulnerable. If people feel that you have come with an objective, something to impose on them, they are less likely to allow themselves to feel tender, reflective or vulnerable.

5

SCIENCE AS ARCHETYPE:
MYTH AS TRUTH

This chapter is devoted to two great stories: science and mythology. These are stories that are both rich in meaning and full of mystery—and that continue to unfold their mysteries as long as we give our loving attention to them. Some would say they are stories that fight with one another. I hope to show here that this is an outdated idea. I marvel at how the two stories often tell the same story in different languages and how the study of both can lead us to the perception of universal archetypes. Becoming conscious of how science is archetypal and the way in which myth speaks truth will help any science interpreter narrow the gap between humans and their engaged perception of the universe.

Every time I give a school performance of myths, a child in the audience will ask me, "Are these stories true?" After years of laboring with long-winded answers, I am satisfied to repeat the words of the Lakota medicine man, Black Elk. He said, "I don't know if it happened exactly that way. But, if you listen to the story long enough, you will hear how it is true." After many years of storytelling, this is still the best answer for those who question the relationship of myths and truth.

Years ago, I became bored with this question and its predicable occurrence at the end of each school assembly. I even became secretly annoyed by children who asked it. "Boy," I thought, "the dominant culture is so hopelessly literal and materialistic in its thinking. If we can't measure it, record it or put our hand on it, we can't understand something as truth. We are training our children to be illiterates in the language of metaphor and symbol. In our efforts to educate children about the world of the practical and the concrete, we are producing illiterates of the imagination."

Then came the shift; I became charmed by the very thing that had annoyed me. It occurred to me that even though I had just told the children a story filled with fantastical monsters and events, they never would have trusted me if I told them, "Yes, the story is all true. It happened just that way." But they still asked. Why did they persist in asking? Some children will even repeat the question two or three times although another has already asked it. I believe that children intuitively know that there is truth in the story. They just don't know how to name or articulate it. They want a little discussion about it, hence the question.

As I explained in chapter 2, the common modern use of the word "myth" connotes a story containing false or outdated beliefs. We often hear some speaker say, "It is time to dispel the old myth that ... ." It has been said that "religion" is what we call our own people's mythology, and "myth" is the term we use for other people's religions—those we don't understand or accept. For this reason, some Native Americans have felt offended by the use of the word "mythology" when referring to the stories of their religion. Because of its modern misuse, the words "myth" and "mythology" give the connotation that their stories are somehow less valuable and not true, and that the people telling and retelling them are naive for doing so. Modern Pagans should equally object to the terms "Celtic mythology" and "Norse mythology." Somewhere there is a group of Greeks practicing the Elysian Mysteries ceremonies, and for them we would have to abandon the term "Greek mythology." Myth is a kind of story that speaks to the sacred and is associated with religious practice. This is why I define myths as *true stories that might have never happened*. Actually, I am not interested if they ever did happen, in the newspaper sense, that is. In essence, they are happening constantly in the lives of all human beings and the forces of the world.

The modern misuse of the word "myth" dismembers a legitimate and very ancient way of speaking about truth. When a presenter speaks a myth, he or she is attempting to communicate truth through a series of allegories, symbols, metaphors and personifications. For some audiences, this form of communication will feel very direct and for others it will be dismissed as nonsense. Either way, the images of a well-told myth will plant themselves in the minds of the audience, like a seed, ready to reveal its truth at a later moment. We can understand this better when we remember that communication through printed language and published text is a recent phenomenon in the history of civilization. How did ancient wisdom keepers hope to preserve truths about creation, death, regeneration, biological life systems and human relationships? I propose that they created (or received through visions) stories that were rich in imagery and allegory—stories that would stick to the imagination. Nobody knows where myths came from. Some suppose that they were received by shamans through dreams. Anyone who has worked with dreams knows that our dream mind is very fluent in this mythical vocabulary of symbol, metaphor and allegory. Carried in this familiar fluid of dream imagery, myths could be remembered and handed down by word of mouth for centuries, until they were written down in text like parts of the Bible and the Grimm fairy tales.

In ancient mythology, there is no separation between the functions of the natural world, which we delineate as biology, chemistry, physics, geology and astronomy, and the function of the divine. In a sense, religion and science were one. In fact, observable scientific functions were often lifted by early myth weavers as readily available metaphors and symbols for expressing the divine. What may seem obvious to us is how myth expresses something about moral truth. What is less obvious is how myth expresses scientific truth.

The purist scientist studies the world of natural phenomena as the devoted monk, priestess or rabbi studies the symbols and allegories of their religion's sacred stories (myth). As both begin to explore the mysterious elements of their story, they find amazing patterns of truth unfolding. Like a child who opens, in delight, another window each day on the advent calendar, both the scientist and the scholar of sacred story notice more and more wisdom in their story the longer they work with it. Over long hours of research and years of experience, both become storytellers. They begin to realize how their story changes and becomes enriched by how their understanding of the story elements grows more complex. As the story's complexity slowly grows inside of them, they recognize that their stories are sacred and they feel a responsibility to carry the story to its fullest expression of truth as they, the storytellers, know it.

In this way, we, the students of sacred story—be it myth or science—may notice that the Greek myth of Demeter and Persephone (the central myth of the Elysian Mysteries) is not only about a mother losing her daughter and a daughter's initiation into womanhood, it is also about the intimate relationship between death and the regeneration of life. After all, the Goddess of Life (Demeter) and the Goddess of Death (Persephone) are mother and daughter—and by the end of the story, the cycle of the seasons is established. A well-worn theme among nature interpreters is the importance of death and decay in an ecosystem. Without death, there would be no new life. This theme is equally popular in the mythology (religious stories) and folktales of every culture. Jack, of "Jack and the Bean Stalk" fame, decides to trick Old Man Death from taking his grandmother in the Scottish folktale, "Death in a Nut." Begrudgingly, Jack has to release Old Man Death when he discovers that without Death nothing in the world moves. Several Native American tribes have a Coyote Story in which Coyote brings death into the world. Confidently, Coyote assures the disappointed animal peoples that without death, the world would become ruined by overpopulation. When Coyote's own daughter is the first one to die, Coyote tries to reverse the way he made things. No such luck, Coyote. Coyote, like many other mythic characters, always helps to remind us how it feels when human nature butts heads with the natural course of things.

In Norse mythology, the importance of the life and death relationship is set forth in the story of creation. During the creation, the great tree of life, Ygdrasil, sprouts toward the heavens. Ygdrasil is a great mythic tree—often referred to as "the World Tree." At once, it is symbolic of spiritual as well as biological truths.

Ygdrasil climbed so high into the heavens that only in the deepest, darkest night can you truly understand her greatness. The stars, even the tiniest of stars that you can see, are hanging on the upper branches of Ygdrasil.

And far below, deep, deep down into the dark earth, Ygdrasil sends her roots. There are three roots. One stretches into the realm of Erda, the Goddess of Life, from which all things are nourished and blossom. Fairies sprinkle dew from her sweet waters every morning to keep the tree's leaves green.

To the other side, the tree bears a more painful burden than mortals can conceive. Into Niefel-heim, the root stretches and takes up waters from its icy cold fountain. There lives the corpse-eating dragon, Nidhog, who gnaws constantly on the life force of the tree. Age rots the root and a multitude of creatures gnaw at the twist through its tender fibers. For ne'er was there good to which evil came not—nor growth without decay.

In the center, a root, white as light, stretches down, down into the well of all memory and the home of Mimir—the God of Memory. Deep in this dark rooty realm, Mimir keeps company with a multitude of little black men who regenerate the world. They are busy, busy, busy, always making a special mead. It is said that any mere mortal who passes through the forest and gathers into their senses the sweet smell of this mead as it sifts up through the soil will become so intoxicated with the divine that words will fall forth from them as if from the mouth of the first creator. And poetry is born.

Up and down the tree runs Ratatosk, the squirrel, who is busy, busy, too. Carrying messages, gossip and news from the realms above to those far below and back again and again … .

There you have it! The symbolic tree of life embodies decay as well as growth—the essence of the nutrient cycle. These primitive Scandinavians intuited, observed and understood what modern scientists struggle to prove, describe or quantify.

Let's take a closer look at this image of Ygdrasil. Certainly, there is more to this image than a single piece of information about the importance of decay. Ygdrasil is a perfect example of what I described earlier as the interfacing of the spiritual and biological. I will delineate these aspects as I see them. This does not mean that I will say all there is to be said about Ygdrasil or have completely defined the tree archetype. Ygdrasil is an archetype of the world tree. An archetype is an image that conveys the universal essence of its own type and nature, no matter what culture produces it. The Madonna or great mother is an example of an archetype. An image of a "great mother" appears in the mythology of all cultures as does the "world tree." As the Swiss psychologist Carl G. Jung said, ultimately, one can never completely explain an archetype. Every myth has at least one archetype, and it is the foundation stone of the myth's meaning. An archetype seems to constantly radiate various shades of meaning the longer we work with its myth. We feel the meanings of an archetype more easily through its imagery than through explanation. Still, I will point out some of the world tree's aspects. (See Strephon K. Williams, *The Jungian-Senoi Dreamwork Manual,* 1985.)

Let's look at the archetype biologically. Ygdrasil makes movement in two broad but related directions. First, we hear of her upper limbs reaching into the sky ("The stars hang on her highest limbs"). Even in the darkness of night, light is associated with her upper limbs. This is clearly one of the functions of trees' upper limbs—to translate light into sugar. The other is to translate atmosphere into matter. Eighty percent of a tree's substance is made from translating the carbon in the air (carbon dioxide) into the solid matter we call wood. In the imagery of the myth, the upper limbs almost seem like a root system in the heavens—in the atmosphere.

Ygdrasil's other direction of movement is into the darkness of earth. Here, we hear about the decaying and generative powers of the roots. Like its branches, those roots of the sky, the ground roots are great translators, too—changing their surroundings and producing gifts for the world in the form of wood, cloth, nuts or fruit.

And what about that central root, "white as light" and all those black dwarfs? Who are they? I once heard the famous ecologist, Dr. Jerry Franklin, speak about old-growth forest systems. He said that for years foresters kept talking about the soil—how they had to fortify the soil and what the soil did for the trees. "My God," said Jerry. "It's not what the soil does for the trees. It's what the trees do for the soil." He continued, "Trees are phenomenal translators of energy. They send all that sugar down into the roots and the mycorrhizae go wild. It's like the tree is sending white light down into the earth!" How amazing that both an ecologist and a myth would use the same image. Mead, which is the mythic drink of the gods, is made from honey—sugar. I would suggest that these black dwarfs are mycorrhizae. The mycorrhizae dwarfs are nourished by the tree's sugar and, in return, nourish the tree with minerals and water. Remember that Ratatosk, the squirrel, is busy carrying messages between both realms. "Any mere mortal" who has gathered an understanding of the dwarfs' mead into their senses and the cycle of life that originated from sunlight can speak a bit of the divine. The gifts of the tree are brought into being by the cooperative efforts of heaven and earth. What has all this to do with Mimir and his well of memory? It has already become evident in poorly managed clear-cuts in the Northwest rain forests. There, where the mycorrhizal life has been exposed to broiling by the sun in clear-cuts, newly planted seedlings forget how to grow. No tree can thrive without its little black dwarfs and Mimir's well of memory. There are many taxa, besides mycorrhizae, that support the life of trees. Ecologist Jerry Franklin refers to this body of creatures and their ecological relationship to trees as "the forest's biological legacy." The "legacy" is certainly the forest's memory.

Slipping into the spiritual, now, this entire story can become a reflection upon wisdom. The name Ygdrasil is derived from the ancient term "ygg," which means ego or self. How is it possible for a human being to develop a strong sense of self and purpose in this world without the support of memory? Think of how fortified our goodness or badness is by the stories of our ancestors. Are we this tall-standing, beautiful being of our own will, alone, or can we remember the multitude of small, obscure beings or events that contributed to what we are? Is our maturation not a long process of blossom and decay, death and regeneration? Finally, what do we translate from the lofty, idealistic, intangible and unseeable into the concrete creations of our work on earth? These are some human contemplations that are modeled by the life efforts of a tree. How wise we become when we see how much like a tree we are.

As the Buddhist saying goes, "The tree grows slowly, but the earth is patient." Ygdrasil was generated out of a Pagan culture, yet as an archetype, it appears in the imagery of all major world religions. In the Christian image, the cross is often referred to as the "tree of life." Through Christ's sacrifice upon the tree, God's light is translated into a kind of sugar (love) on earth. In Buddhism, Buddha received his first revelations through the tree of life under which he sat in meditation. In many folk stories from Asia and other parts of the world, characters receive special wisdom while sitting under a tree.

FINDING THE ARCHETYPE IN MYTHIC AND SCIENTIFIC RESEARCH

As we have seen in the story of Ygdrasil, an archetype carries a lot of different information about beings, environments and processes. Our understanding and research of any myth's archetype is always enhanced by the study of that archetype in as many myths as possible. Although Jung said that an archetype can never be ultimately explained, extensive study of multicultural myths of a particular natural archetype will reveal many facets of that archetype's biological characteristics. Through such a study, we can begin to see a relationship between scientific and spiritual wisdom.

The wolf archetype, for instance, reveals four distinct qualities found in any world myth that contains wolf characters. I identify these qualities or sub-archetypes as the following:

1. **The Devoted Parent**
   Mythic image: Many great heroes are reputed to have been raised by wolves who come in a time of need and nurture the human as devotedly as if it were a human mother—maybe with even greater devotion. Some include: Romulus and Remus, the founders of Rome; Alexander the Great; and King Cyrus, the founder of the Persian Empire.
   Biological quality: Wolves are known to defend their pups to the death against invading grizzly bears or risk being shot to rescue their pups from human captors.

2. **The Swallowing One, Death or Predator**
   Mythic image: Skoll and Hati from Nordic myth who keep all life on earth moving because they chase the sun and moon across the sky. They represent the advent of death, which is always possible and keeps time moving and all life active, alert, healthy and vibrant.
   Biological quality: Predators are essential in keeping prey animal populations healthy and active by culling the weak and sick.

3. **Loyal Pack Member**
   Mythic image: In Native American, Russian and Japanese myths, the wolf is always true to its word and loyal to its human partner to the end. This same quality of loyalty to clan, which domesticated dogs have inherited from wolves, is the quality that humans seem to appreciate most about the dog as a pet.
   Biological quality: Wolves mate for life, hunt and raise their young communally and are loyal to their pack members.

4. **Spirit Guide and Resourceful Survivor**
   Mythic image: In many world myths, the wolf is the animal most connected to the mysterious element of life. It is the animal that knows the way out of the fairy tale's "dark forest" and the secrets for surviving near-death circumstances.
   Biological quality: Wolves are extremely strong and intelligent and, once injured, have amazing powers to heal.

Not only can we learn something scientific about the wolf from studying its mythology, but we can also learn something about how to tell its scientific story. Notice that two of the qualities are related to death and two are related to devotion. Death and devotion are two very powerful subjects. These four sub-archetypes, more simply stated as "death and devotion," give us important interpretive themes around which to organize scientific information for an interpretive presentation. In hundreds of random interviews with people who are fascinated by wolves, I have discovered that these wolf admirers are deeply moved by some piece of scientific information that fits into one of these sub-archetype categories. In telling science as a story with fascination, it is essential to realize that there is something archetypal flowing through the raw information. Our job as interpreters is to keep searching for the various facets of that archetype.

With enough research, one no longer has to believe that mythology and science have to be at war with one another. Generally speaking, when one goes back to the uncensored recordings of indigenous people's myths, in every continent, one will find mythic representations of nature that metaphorically illustrate biological, geological and mathematical concepts.

MYTHS IN CONFLICT WITH SCIENCE

Before discussing more examples of these myths, let's detour for a moment to acknowledge the existence of myths that illustrate a separation between mythic and scientific truth. These stories have been generated primarily by religious/political institutions that have either sought to control their constituency through fear or ennoble the human being by debasing the value of nature—or by fable or folktale tellers who simplify the characteristics of an animal into an anthropomorphic projection for the purpose of making a moral point about human nature.

The wolf, the snake, the pig and the bear have all suffered from this myth abuse. It is evident how devastating the false myths of the wolf have been. Wolves are extinct or close to extinction in many parts of their former range, and some people still believe that they will attack and eat humans. Although this unjust falsehood is being changed through the educational efforts of many conservation groups, the magnitude of the struggle is testimony to the power of myth. The heaviest blow came to the wolf in the Dark Ages of Europe, when the Catholic Church associated the wolf with heretics. This association quickly led to an alignment of the wolf with the devil. As I described earlier in this chapter and in more depth in my book, *Wolf Stories: Myths and True Life Tales from Around the World* (1993), wolves never acquired this kind of negative image in other world cultures. Pre– and post–Dark Ages stories show this change from a wolf as a heroic spirit guide in ancient Russian fairy tales such as "The Firebird, Prince Ivan and the Wolf" into the appearance of the Big Bad Wolf in "Little Red Riding Hood" and "Peter and the Wolf" (a story invented by Russian composer Prokofiev). Most European fairy tales show remnant aspects of more ancient Greek, Celtic, Germanic and Egyptian myths. "Little Red Riding Hood" is completely original, however, and has no earlier root story. It first appeared in European folklore during the Inquisition.

Snakes have suffered equally by association with the devil. Like the wolf, not all cultures have given the snake a demon's role in their mythology. Ironically, in

India, where some of the world's most dangerous snakes live, the snake is revered as a symbol of the life force or Kundalini. In a dream or myth, a snake bite represents the life force trying to enter and awaken the soul. In many world cultures, the snake swallowing its tail or shedding its skin represents eternal life. In a Flathead (Native American) myth, Rattlesnake saves the people from a skeleton-head monster by removing his poisonous fangs and putting them into a pot of stew that will be eaten by the monster. In many Native American tribes, the snake is the messenger from the underworld as birds are the messengers from the upper world. Both worlds are equally divine. The spirit beings of each world provide wisdom and medicines that are equally beneficial to this world, although they are different. One of the important medicines brought by the snake is water.

In the mythic/spiritual worldviews of Native American tribes, all life forms are an essential and honored part of the creation—especially the small and ugly. This is often true of indigenous cultures. In the pre-Judeo-Christian Goddess religions of the Mediterranean, snakes, along with doves, were honored in the temples through art and ceremonial uses. It is believed that poisonous snakes were milked and that their poison was used to induce the altered states of the female priestesses who performed the function of oracles. Today, doctors are experimenting with snake poisons as an aid in decreasing cholesterol. In modern science, as in the old myths, one should never underestimate the special gifts or usefulness of small, ugly or dangerous creatures.

In one's research, it is important to uncover the earliest "root" myths or variations on a myth so as to avoid passing on a false archetype. Also, it is important not to confuse mythic story, such as fairy tale, myth or sacred text, with folktales or fables. As stated earlier, folktales and fables usually misrepresent an animal for the purpose of creating a drama about human nature. Whereas mythic stories identify and reveal a more sophisticated observation of an animal's nature through the archetype, folktales and fables project human qualities on the animal. For instance, in most folktales and fables, the bear plays the role of the stupid one who is always tricked. Whereas in many indigenous myths, the bear is connected with healing, plant medicines and the recovery of power through long sleep or a kind of social hibernation. The bear is revered, not a stupid animal at all, but a source of medicinal knowledge, mysterious healing powers and strength—in addition to being the sire of kings.

The story of King Arthur, for example, is said to have evolved from an ancient Suomi (Native northern Scandinavian) myth about a woman who marries a bear and gives birth to a son who is half man and half bear (Sacred Paw). In the Suomi myth, the boy is injured by other boys who are jealous of his strength. The Bear Son retreats deep into a cave and journeys into the underworld where he sleeps for a year. After he is healed, he leaves the cave with renewed strength and vanquishes his enemies. In the story of King Arthur, the name "Arthur" means bear. The time when young King Arthur was under the tutelage of Merlin and the mysterious "Ladies of the Lake" is considered a kind of hibernation stage through which his strength as an enlightened king was fostered.

Often in folktales, the domesticated animal is the model for the character, whereas in mythology, the wild animal is the model. Contrast, for example, the frightened, unintelligent weaklings of "The Three Little Pigs" fame and the wild, angry boar that jealous Mars (Greco-Roman god of War) becomes when he gores Venus' lover, Adonis. Or what about Kama-Puaa, the Hog-god of Hawaiian myth who is the only god that manages to seduce the easily angered fire goddess, Pele? He accomplishes this rare feat by wile. There is nothing weak or stupid about his persona.

I am not suggesting that we ignore all myths that present negative attitudes toward nature. Certainly, one should be wary of particular snakes, and wildfire can clearly be a kind of hell. Still, it is important to notice that elements of nature and animals that have suffered from the negative images of some mythologies are represented for their positive aspects in other mythologies. Wildfire, for instance, is symbolically represented by huge bonfires set by the Celts during their spring festival of Betane to symbolize the cleaning and rejuvenating powers of fire. They marched their cattle between the bonfires to signify agricultural health and the fire's power to subdue botanical and insect-related diseases. As the saying goes, "There are two sides to every story," and there are many more than two to every archetype. All stories are part of the complete research that has to be done in order to fully explore an archetype. You need not feel that you have to present the negative stories, only that you are aware of them. Certainly, the snake and the wolf are due for a little tilting of the balance since they have suffered so long under negative stories.

Have patience and humility. This kind of research can take years before the fullness of the archetype begins to flower. When you are exploring archetypes in mythic or scientific story, what you are actually looking for are patterns or deeper currents of meaning. What this exploration gives your storytelling, whether you are telling myths or scientific fact as a story, is a way of knowing—knowing the important pictures in your story and how to organize them. I cannot emphasize it enough: Images carry the essential meaning of any story. They are the central nervous system of the story.

GEOLOGICAL AND MATHEMATICAL MYTHIC IMAGERY

We have seen some examples of how indigenous people's myths metaphorically illustrate biological concepts. Let's continue to explore myth's way of speaking truth through image in stories that illustrate some geological and mathematical concepts.

Once upon a time, I told the creation myth of a band of the Pawnee, called the Skidi, at a science museum in Michigan. Here is a part of it:

Before there was earth ... before the dawn ... before there was light ... there was Tirawa, the great creating one ... and Tirawa was calling across the heavens ... calling the spirits along the sky path ... calling the Powers of the Four Directions, calling them all together in one great creation council. Together they began to sing ... singing and shaking their rattles. And as they sang, winds began to whip across the heavens ... winds whipped up clouds ... clouds gathered in deep, dark pools. And then, Tirawa took a rose quartz pebble and dropped it. Easily, it fell in among the clouds ... and then the Lightning and Thunder beings struck right through the rose quartz. The storm began to subside. The clouds split and dispersed ... and below the creators of heaven was a vast ocean ... . (from Strauss, *Wolf Stories: Myths and True Life Stories from Around the World,* 1993). Also, on tape, Strauss, *Coyote Gets a Cadillac and Other Eye-Opening Earth Tales,* 1991, and on video, *Mythic Wolf.*

After the telling, a man came up from the audience breathless and said, "That story! That story! It's the big bang theory ... but ... but ... it's a myth!" He understood the picture beyond the literal meaning of the words.

Another time, I told the Skidi Pawnee creation story along with two other creation myths: the Nordic creation myth and one I had created out of several of my own dream sequences and interviews with a geologist. My performance was followed by a "talk" by Forest Service geologist Larry Chitwood at a celebration for the Newberry National Volcanic Monument. I mention the specifics of this performance situation because it was such a rewarding interpretive experience for the Forest Service geologists, who had never heard geology told in mythic form, and for the public, who received the benefit of hearing geological story reinforced in two languages—so to speak. Here are some parts from the Nordic myth:

That long, long, long ago ... in the ages when naught else was, there yawned in space a vast gulf of nothingness called Ginnungap. Ginnungap ... Ginnungap ... it hung like a windless summer day ... Ginnungap. Its length was immeasurable ... its breath was immeasurable and its depth was beyond all comprehension.

But on one far end was Nifel-heim. Aah! Nifel-heim, the realm of icy, misty darkness and freezing cold. Aah! Nifel-heim, where twelve rivers run of icy venomous vapors ... layer upon layer, the ice heaps up in fantastic forms one above another. Thick vapors envelop the icy forms and whirlwinds scream in horror within them.

And far to the other end, is Muspel-heim. Aah! Muspel-heim, the luminous home of fire and light. Aah! Muspel-heim, it glows with rivers of molten rock and moving fire. Sparks of shining fire free themselves from their home ... yearning toward the empty space.

And there in time ... in Ginnungap ... where the realm of tempests and gloom met the realm of warmth and light ... it was there and then, when the first sparks of fire flew to the frozen ice that the first drop of water formed and all life began ... drip ... drip ... drip ... .

... After the Asa-Gods had defeated the Ice-Giants, they killed Ymer (father of the Ice-Giants) and spilled out his icy cold blood, which became the oceans of the world. They took his bones to make the mountains of the world and broke his jaw ... throwing his teeth along the shores, which are the boulders you see strewn here and there near the sea.

Then, they threw his body onto the great World Mill. Do you know about the great World Mill? It sits deep below in the ocean floor and it is churned by nine giant maidens with braids made of white light. Turning and churning, the great World Mill ground Ymer's body and spewed it forth ... making the lands of the earth and the sands near the seas. And, every time you feel the earth tremble and quake, it is the nine giant maidens, they are throwing another Ice-Giant upon the World Mill.

After my part of the program, Larry took his place on the stage, paused for a few moments and then said, "Ah—yes, well it's kind of like Susan just said—all that churning and turning and grinding—very slowly—very slowly." Later, backstage, Larry found his perfect metaphor for volcanic events in the geological time line. "It's like a gamelan orchestra," he said. The gamelan is an Indonesian orchestra of multisized bells. Each player plays his or her bells in a distinct, particular pattern of timing, which interfaces with the patterns of other players. The music creates a sound that is a kind of representation of all life interacting. One player may hit his or her bell only once in a two-hour performance, or not at all. This player represents occurrences in the world that happen only once in a very long cycle—such as geological events. The purpose of this bell player is to remind us of the magnitude of time in the movement of creative forces. With this metaphor and image, Larry stepped into the realm of telling scientific fact as story.

Creation myths are marvelous creatures in their own right. There is so much that can be learned from them. Why not? After all, creation is at the core of all aspects of life. There is heterosexual creation; asexual creation; the creative process of a committee; creation that requires an environment of conflict, strife, attraction or peacefulness; the mystery of how chlorophyll molecules create sugar from light and the grand mysteries of how life on earth first began. All of these aspects of the creation archetype are communicated through the various creation myths of the world.

Often this communication occurs through the most mysterious language of archetype: mathematics. In the modern world, we use numbers so frequently for matters of commerce and statistics that we forget they are essentially symbols. As symbols, numbers create images. In the ancient world, numbers were another language for telling a story. Upon reading a variety of world creation myths, you will discover an abundance of references to the numbers one and especially two. One represents the archetype of unity, wholeness or the original divine source, which then begins a dividing or multiplying. Sometimes the one begins by presenting itself as a two, as in the incidence of the "twin brothers." These twins, one good and one bad, begin the creation in the Mayan creation myth, the Popoh Vul. The Quesan, Natives to the American Southwest, also begin with two contrary twin brothers. These conflicting brothers don't appear immediately in the Jewish Torah's story of Genesis, but they show up soon after in the form of Adam and Eve or Cain and Abel. In the Buddhist sacred text, *Tao Te Ching*, "the one" is constantly described as a dance between dualities.

> *The way that can be spoken of*
> *Is not the constant way;*
> *The name that can be named*
> *Is not the constant name.*
> *The nameless was the beginning of heaven and earth;*
> *The named was the mother of the myriad creatures.*
> *Hence always rid yourself of desires in order to observe its secrets;*
> *But always allow yourself to have desires in order to observe*
> *its manifestations.*
> *These two are the same*
> *But diverge in name as they issue forth.*
> *Being the same they are called mysteries,*
> *Mystery upon mystery—*
> *The gateway of the manifold secrets.*
>
> (FROM LAO-TZU, *TAO TE CHING*, 1963)

In the Nordic creation, two realms, one of fire and the other of ice, two opposites, slowly move toward each other in the emptiness of space. At the moment they meet, the first drop of water forms, and in this water, the first life-form begins to take shape. Once a Swedish man excitedly reported this story to me and said, "It's right there in the beginning! There, where the contrasts meet ... . Bang! There is life!" (I am eternally grateful to him, for he opened up my fascination for the entire subject of Nordic mythology with that one comment.) In this image of two, or the sacred duality, we see a picture of what I described earlier as "creation that requires an environment of conflict." The

Upanishad creation myth begins with one being who is lonely. Out of loneliness, the one creates another (two). When they couple, they create birds. They are so delighted with the beauty of their creation that they continue to couple and create all of the creatures of the world (an image of "creation" that requires an environment of attraction). In the beginning for the Mandan, Natives of the North American plains, both Lone Man and First Creator make the world together. At one point in the story, First Creator changes himself into Coyote and continues to make the world ready for the human beings. At times, in other Coyote Stories, Coyote foolishly ends up in trouble. Then Fox appears as Coyote's younger brother to help him out or bring him back to life if he has died. Fox acts like another form of Lone Man or the twin brother. These are the many pictures of two.

The number three can represent the two instruments of creation plus their outcome or the concept of completion—as in the completion of a cycle of creation. With the number three, we progress from the concepts of unity and twin/ contrast to cycle in which there is a sense of movement or time. In the pre-Judeo-Christian Goddess religions, cycles represent a basic pattern of all life. We see this pattern in the phases of human life: maiden, matron and crone, or boy, father and grandfather. In Christianity, three represents the Holy Trinity: Father, Son and Holy Spirit. In either instance, three describes a story that demonstrates a unity in its three phases. It is a story that has time like all biological life cycles— the beginning of new life, harvest and death (or the return).

Depending on the culture, four represents a balance or stabilizing of polar opposites: a relationship between the heavenly and earthly domains as in the Christian cross and the northern European Pagan world tree, an acknowledgment of the powers of creation in the entire universe as honored in the four directions of medicine wheels found in Native American, African, Celtic and Asian traditions. The stability of the square (first possible to draw with four points) is distinct from the fluidity and motion of a circle (first possible to draw with three points). Honored by Pythagoras' mysteries teachings, geometry was studied as a way to reach the divine.

The addition of three and four makes seven. The multiplication of three times four makes twelve. Seven and twelve are two numbers that communicate the idea of perfection through many cultures. There are seven notes in the major scale. When we hit the octave note, it expresses a sound in unity with the first note and the concept of harmony is born. There are five notes in the minor scale. The contrasting major and minor tones make twelve altogether ... and so there is the creation of an experience we call music. In Genesis, God makes the world in seven days. Snow White's perfection is first noticed by her evil stepmother's mirror when she turns seven years old. She has to travel over seven hills and seven valleys before she can find refuge with the seven dwarfs. The

Babylonian spiritual teacher, Zarathustra, identified twelve celestial forces he said impacted creation on earth. Later, these became known as the constellations of the Sidereal zodiac. The molecular structure of a chlorophyll molecule forms a twelve-pointed star. This is the molecule that transforms light into the basis for all organic life on earth. All of the above show telling stories with numbers.

An old college friend went from an undergraduate degree in literature to a doctorate in mathematics. When I asked her why, she said, "Well, there is just so much wisdom in the story that math tells." Again, we return to that important word in chapter 1: relationship. My friend became devoted to an in-depth study of mathematics because of its archetypes or, in other words, the deeper current of truth within the language of mathematics. For my friend, mathematical information is fascinating for no other reason than it has relationship to a more universal truth she called "wisdom." Once again, we can hear echoes of John Keats' proclamation:

> *Beauty is truth, truth beauty—that is all*
> *Ye know on earth, and all ye need to know.*

When we are talking about mathematics, geology, ecology or physics with relationship, archetypal truth and image in mind, we are creating story.

6

TELLING SCIENTIFIC FACT AS STORY

Doing your research and ruminating about the archetypal patterns in your scientific or historic facts is like the activity of a gardener who prepares the soil for spring flowers. All sorts of possible stories may sprout from this fertile soil. In this chapter, I have set forth as many examples of these flowers as I have observed. Each identifies a kind of story structure that can give you a jump start on creating your own stories. As always, consider these models as training wheels and inspiration—not recipes. An audience's interest will falter if people feel you are speaking out of a recipe rather than out of your own, well-researched and original passion. Remember, finding a story that works for you is not unlike the image of Cinderella's prince searching the kingdom for the foot that will fit the glass slipper. If a story structure feels too much like you've had to cut off your toes and heal to fit into it, you may need to do some more ruminating or choose another. Some structures just may not suit your style.

ANECDOTE/SCIENTIFIC INFORMATION WEAVE

Find an anecdote that gives expression to an archetype that is also found in some scientific information. When the scientific information is woven through the course of the anecdote, the archetype, now reflecting between human experience and scientific thought, becomes pronounced and the scientific information is more memorable.

I list this structure first because anecdotes feel most natural to beginning interpreter/tellers and can make a strong and lasting impression on their audiences. This is true because everyone has experiences that support their knowledge, and sharing experiences is something human beings do all the time. With regard to this structure, I'm just asking that a bit more interpretive/artistic consciousness be brought to the activity. Also, because an anecdote is such a conversational form of storytelling, it disarms an audience's guardedness. Despite the interpreter/

artist consciousness you bring to your anecdote making, the audience should still hear it as just a story or a "by the way, this happened to me once" experience instead of as a lesson or instruction. Anecdotes are very useful during casual interpretive presentations, such as nature walks or talks in front of museum exhibits, because they are short. The teaching power of this form comes out of the simple and clean way it creates relationship between that which is human and that which is scientific. Most people view the natural and human worlds as separate entities. As Carl Sagan has pointed out on many occasions, we are currently living in a time when human life is increasingly influenced by the discoveries of complex scientific processes, and yet the average person is ignorant of the most simple of scientific processes. This is a dangerous situation. During radio or television interviews about the old-growth forest issue, I have heard members of the public speak with anger about how some government policy was placing science above humans. I think to myself, Do they actually believe that science can be separated from people? Do they not turn on light switches? Do they not want to drink clean water? Do they not want to eat healthy fish? Through this form, we see how science impacts our human lives—that we are science—that life is science. The following example story is from my performance: *Secrets from the Dark Forest: Tree Stories.* The second story is from Roberta Hilbruner, my former student and chief of interpretation for the Columbia Gorge National Scenic Area.

Good Bob, Bad Bob

Growing up, I remember hearing my father say, "The reason why it says in the Bible to love thy neighbor is because it's such a damn hard thing to do."

So it must have been no mistake that when I came to settle down in Bend—the place I wanted to plant my roots, the place I wanted to call home—that I found I was living between two Bobs. Good Bob and Bad Bob.

Now, the Bob who lives between us and our beautiful view of the Three Sisters Mountains is an angry older man who always talks like the world owes him a favor. Once when he was angry that my husband was too busy to help him with a repair, he threatened to build his new barn in front of our view of the mountains. That's when we named him Bad Bob.

The Bob who lives to the south of us is a very religious man. He is of the same religious affiliation as Bad Bob, but he expresses his beliefs in every one of his good deeds. He is a man who "walks his talk," as a Native friend of mine is used to saying. He supplies us with any help he can provide, if we need it. He translates the love that he receives from his god and makes a kind of energy or sugar from it. We feel supported—like, we can breath a little easier—and go about our business in the world because we have Bob as a neighbor. We call him Good Bob.

The other day Good Bob called to see how I was—he usually does—just shortly before I had to catch a plane. In a hurried voice I thanked him for his concern and then thought that he might be interested in where I was going. I said, "Hey, Bob, I'm going to tell stories about prayer and vision for a conference of environmental educators in the Midwest!"

I thought he would be interested, but he was silent. Then he asked, "Well, how do environmentalists pray?"

I was a little stunned. I said, "Well, I guess it depends on whether they're Jewish or Christian or Buddhists or whatever."

"I mean," he said, "if evolution was your god, who would you pray to?"

"Evolution isn't a god, Bob," I said. "Evolution is one of the phenomenal processes that God made."

He was silent on the other end of the line. I continued, "The creation is filled with these extraordinary processes." Bob was silent. "Like trees," I continued. "Trees are a living, breathing, spiritual fact." I was sure he would get my meaning, but Bob was silent. "Bob," I said, "trees lift their leaves to the sun and make sugar out of sunlight. Can you lift your hand to the sun and do that? They are a miracle." Bob was silent. "They are incredible translators. Eighty percent of the tree's body, that part that we used to build our houses, is translated out of the air. Eighty percent of the tree's body is made from carbon and it breathes in that carbon from the atmosphere." Bob was still silent. Feeling that I might be losing my audience, I continued with increased passion.

"Bob, trees provided homes, nuts, seeds and fruits for hundreds of other creatures as well as for us. Even when they are dead, they are providing homes—and food. They are incredible givers. They send sugar down into their roots to feed mycorrhizae, which in turn help transport water and minerals back up into the tree—and without these mycorrhizae, seedling trees could not get started or survive—and then, mycorrhizae bloom into truffles that feed voles, which in turn feed spotted owls. Bob, trees translate the gifts of heaven for the earthly domain. Bob, trees are good neighbors—like you Bob, the tree is a good neighbor.

PHILIP'S STORY

My son Philip blew into the house like he always does, dancing about like the tail on the end of a kite. But this day I noticed a difference—he wasn't singing as he hung up his coat and put away his pack.

Now, Philip is a boy who has always had a song in his heart—a song to greet the day—a song to sing his socks on and tune up his cereal—a song to orchestrate his play with the dog—a song for the mirror—and the table—and even the toilet paper! And he has a special song we sing together at bedtime. So if Philip isn't singing I know something is wrong. He hung his head ... .

"Aw, Mom, all the kids were making fun of me again. It's 'cause I'm always singing and I wear 'benders. They call me 'Erkel' and 'Singerman.'"

I picked him up and as we snuggled I wondered how to comfort or counsel him. As I searched for inspiration, my glance caught the wildflower calendar on the wall.

**

The thing that has always fascinated me about wildflowers is how they fit their environment—how they have just the right stuff to survive. In the Columbia Gorge, larkspur doesn't grow in the east—its tall, spiky stem would be flattened in the wind and its fragile leaves desiccated by the sun. It is made tall to reach above the dense forest floor and find the light that filters through the trees. It sinks its roots into the boggy, spongy duff.

Balsam root, however, loves the dry, rocky scablands of the eastern gorge. It grows low to keep out of the wind, and its hairy leaves trap moisture and protect it from the wind.

Stone cup grows in the rocky clefts of the gorge and stores what water it finds in its thick, waxy, succulent leaves.

**

With my mind on fitting in, I asked Philip if he'd like me to get him a belt. He looked at me with his wise, brown, five-year-old eyes. "No, Mom. I like my 'benders—and it's good to be different!"

And I knew that like the White Shooting Star, the relict that has survived in the cool, dark, damp crannies of the gorge since the Ice Age, our little Singerman would also find his own special niche.

OBSERVATIONS/ADVENTURE STORIES

Find a biologist's observation, a daily event in nature (such as a hunt or thunderstorm), or "A Day in the Life of Some Creature," and tell it as an adventure story. "Railroad Coyote" is taken from the observations of Dayton Hyde, a southeast Oregon rancher. I rewrote it for inclusion in my book, *Coyote Stories for Children: Tales from Native America* (1991).

RAILROAD COYOTE

That coyote could be seen ramblin' along the railroad tracks most weekdays about one o'clock in the afternoon. It was a little after one that the train bound for Nevada swept through the valley. That coyote drifted about from side to side as much as he was progressing forward. Coyote kept his nose to the ground as if there were something of interest on that side of the tracks.

On the other side of the tracks, ground squirrels had taken cover in their tunnels under the earth. Far up the tracks, other ground squirrels sat up, out of their holes watching Coyote.

When the train came storming by, Coyote picked up his gait to a full, shotgun gallop. He raced that train until the last car passed—opening the tracks to his view again. He leaped directly over the tracks—much to the surprise of the ground squirrels—and caught one in his mouth. That railroad coyote trick worked again!

"A Wolf at the Door" appears in my book, *Wolf Stories: Myths and True Life Tales from Around the World.* It is the experience of Dr. David Mech. I rewrote it from the following excerpt from Dr. Mech's book, *The Way of the Wolf* (1991). I present both versions of the story here to help illustrate the differences between story making and scientific writing. My version of the story was enhanced through phone conversations with Dr. Mech about his experience. In those conversations, I was searching for any clue that would help inspire me to create in picture and language rhythm what Dr. Mech was stating as scientific fact or observation. Here is Dr. Mech's version:

Wolves show a great breadth of learning ability, even greater than that of dogs ... . Certainly, wolves also seem to be very good at insightful behavior, that is, behavior implying that the wolf might actually understand certain relationships. Once a wolf has learned how to escape from a pen, for example, it is almost impossible to keep the animal in. One such escape artist I knew learned to raise a drop door in its pen by jumping to the top of the 8-foot-high pen, and grabbing with its teeth the door cable on the outside of the pen, which was exposed to the inside through a 3-inch gap. By jumping up and grabbing the cable, the wolf could lift the door at the bottom of the cage. After the wolf raised the door many times, it stuck in the "up" position, and the wolf ran out!

And here is my version:

When a wolf has figured out how to escape from a pen, it won't stay caged for long.

Once, such an escape artist was among a group of wolves being studied by the famous wolf biologist, Dr. David Mech. During the course of their research, Dr. Mech and others often let the wolf out of its cage into a larger pen. The wolf watched as the cage door slid up and down on its cable wires. Up the door would go, and back the cable wire would pull along the 8-foot-high horizon ridge of the pen wall. At one point along the ridge, the wire cable arched, ever so slightly, to the inside of the pen.

The wolf jumped for it and grabbed the cable with its teeth. The door slid up ... and then down ... once the wolf let go of the wire. But the wolf was not discouraged. It repeated the same 8-foot jump and cable-grab again and again until the door stuck ... and the wolf was gone.

"A day in the life of a creature" is another way of looking at this observations/ adventure story form. Here is an excerpt from Salli Nigg's "A Shark's Day." Salli, a former student of mine, teaches in the education department of the Monterey Bay Aquarium.

Shark slips through cool clear waters. Sunlight dances on her sleek powerful body as she moves gracefully through the silence and disappears.

Old gray seal noisily munches on a nice juicy fish as he basked on the ocean surface in the warm summer sun. He had been feasting on fish all morning, but he just couldn't seem to get enough.

Shark slips through cool clear waters. Suddenly, she hears a faint crunching noise from far away. She turns toward the sound and slowly disappears.

Old gray seal was so full! Just when he thought he couldn't eat another bite, he spotted one last little fish hiding behind a rock. "That silly little fish thinks he can hide from me, but I can see him just fine and he looks like the perfect juicy morsel to cleanse my palette," said the old gray seal.

The little fish was frozen, too scared to move. "Don't eat me, don't eat me, don't eat me!" shrieked the little fish.

Crunch! "Ah! Just what I needed. Now I think I'm ready for a little nap," sighed the old gray seal.

Shark slips silently through cool clear waters moving toward the sound. Sniffing in the water, she picks up the faintest scent of blood. The smell draws her closer. She swishes her tail, increasing her speed as she disappears.

Old gray seal is sleepy. He decides to take a little nap on the nearest rock. Old gray seal swims up to the rock and gives a mighty push with his flippers, but he had eaten too much and could not make it onto the rock. He tries again and again to no avail. "Oh well, I'll just bask here on the surface for a bit," yawned the old gray seal.

Shark slips through clear cool waters moving toward the smell. She begins to feel along the sides of her long body tiny movements of water caused by something swimming somewhere in the area. She gazes around her looking for the source.

Old gray seal sleepily rolls onto his belly and looks beneath him as he dozes. Suddenly he freezes. He sees a shark cruising silently near the bottom. "Any minute she's going to see me up here! I'll just sneak down behind her and hide by the rock down there. Why, she won't even see my gray body next to the gray rock." Gray seal waits for shark to pass and quietly sank down to the bottom near the rock.

Shark slips through cool clear waters looking for food. She can smell food and she felt it earlier. Now to locate it. As she passes near a rock, she quickly turns. Something is different. She senses the electricity of something alive!

Old gray seal is holding very still, but he's been holding his breath for a long time. Just when he thinks it's safe to move, shark turns and passes back over seal and the gray rocks. Seal waits and he waits, but the shark seems to be in no hurry to leave, as if she could sense he was there. "I can't stand it anymore! I've got to get out of here!" seal's mind screams to himself. Old gray seal dashes for the surface!

Shark whips her body around as seal darts by and springs into action with her powerful tail!

Old gray seal was almost to the rock, just a few more feet. With one last great effort he launches his fat body into the air, just as the shark's jaws clamped down.

Contrast Point of View

Tell an event from two points of view, that of the human and that of the creature or element. Mary Kline, a former student of mine, works for the National Park Service. She wanted to develop a story about what happens to bears when visitors begin to feed them or leave food out where bears can get to it. Her true story did not have a happy ending. It did have a humorous middle, however, which created a strong contrast to the ending—giving it a greater punch. She also used contrast effectively by having the park ranger constantly refer to the bear by number: "Bear 49148 has been spotted ... " In the story the bear doesn't refer to himself by number, of course, and gives part of the narration from his own perspective:

It was the same campground where people had left food out the year before. I'll just go by and see what's there this year.

I came out of the trees into the meadow. Humans started running around. Two of them were waving their arms around. There was the cooler ... on the table behind them. I went up to the cooler and pushed the human and some bees out of the way.

One of the benefits of this "contrast point of view" form is that it enhances the value of the specific—what Dr. Sam Ham refers to as "focusing on the individual." I have noticed that when human beings give a name to a place or creature, it becomes more valued. For example, once a particular area in the Northwest old-growth forest system gains a name, such as Opal Creek, it gains a greater chance of being preserved. People who have an interest in not preserving a certain area often refer to the area with lot numbers or other nonfamiliar ways of naming.

FACTS CLOTHED IN CENTRAL ARCHETYPE

Tell your facts with a unifying image or central archetype that connects all information related to a subject.

I remember going on a tour of a Headstart Center with its director. Proudly, she pointed out the various places in the rooms where certain activities took place at different times in the daily schedule. Then, she pointed to a lone desk with a plastic microscope and some plastic petri dishes on it. "And that is our science area," she announced. I thought to myself, "How sad science looks over there—so serious with its laboratory instruments—neglected by the five-year-olds—separated from the mainstream of classroom life and all of life, in general."

The following is a story created by Gina O'Brien, my former student and a biologist with the Malheur National Forest. I am particularly fond of this story style because it is such a perfect synthesis of science and story. We, the listeners, fall completely into the spell of the science without realizing we are hearing story—or one might say, we fall completely into the spell of the story without realizing we are hearing science. This is the kind of science teaching that is practiced in Waldorf Schools.

GINA'S SYMPHONY

There is a song in this world that is almost as old as the earth herself. This song is so intricate, so complex, that it confounds the imagination. And the most incredible thing about this song is that it's composed of notes that, by themselves, are often not heard. Notes as quiet and insignificant as a seed pearl of mist.

The most wonderful thing about these notes is that, just by their existence, they create more notes. The notes shivered by a fawn shaking its dew-drenched coat. The notes silvering the new spring grass. The slight, dripping notes falling from the moisture-laden leaves to the rich soil below.

And these notes, in turn, create more notes as they unfurl the fiddleheads and moisten the moss on their trickled trek downhill. When all of these singing notes gather, they form the melody of a stream.

And this melody creates more notes, and more melodies as it flows down its course: the fluting trill of the red-winged blackbird and the laughing battle cry of the kingfisher. And more harmonies ... the silver splash of the cutthroat trout in counterpoint with the deft darting of the dragonfly ... the polite applause of the white-skinned aspen come into concert with the whisper of the tall meadow grasses. And all around, within and throughout these melodies, come more notes that sing of the coyote's quick leap after the white-footed mouse, the harrier hawk's hovering wings and the shrill, shrieking laughter of children from the people who have always lived by the stream. All of these rhythms and melodies intertwined to create a Great Symphony and its harmonies resonated with those of the earth.

Now, not all of these rhythms were pleasant. Sometimes it was a cacophony of flood, but that was part of the symphony. Sometimes it was the dull drone of drought, but that, too, was part of the symphony. And these rhythms were important in maintaining the complexities and intricacies of the whole song.

Then, within a few beats of the earth's heart, something changed. A discordance arose. A new people arrived at the stream. They brought with them a new melody—a simple melody. One that did not harmonize with the melodies of the stream.

Now these people were not wicked or evil. They did not strive to create discord or to disrupt the harmony. The sad fact is that they did not hear the harmony and did not know how to blend with it. Oh, they heard the notes, and some even heard the simpler melodies. Many would go out of their way to listen and enjoy them, but rarely did they look upon these notes as part of the Great Symphony. The new people saw the notes and melodies as something to use to strengthen their own song, and the people used them to that end.

The melody of the new people was not a bad melody. In many ways, it had its own beauty, with very simple tunes and many single notes— notes of the golden grainfields waving in the wind, a newborn calf staggering to its mother or tidy gardens. These were good melodies, and they were the songs that their parents and grandparents had bestowed on them. And because they were given with love and had the secure comfort of familiarity, this song played sweet and loud and strong in the ears of the new people.

So when they took the notes of water to play their melodies of crops and gardens, they didn't notice the melodies of the aspen or dragonfly grew weak. When their cattle played their tunes in the meadows by the stream, no one noticed that the tune of the grasses became clipped and strained. And as the melodies weakened, so too did the notes. The cutthroat trout and the kingfisher no longer had the full-throated stream to sing with. The clipped notes of grass could no longer hold the tune of the mouse or the rabbit, and the notes of coyote and harrier hawk became few and scattered. And as the notes and the tunes became fewer and more muted, the melodies became less intricate, and the harmony was no longer tightly woven.

When the rhythm of flood or fire or drought moved through the land, the song could no longer stretch and fill its score, and the song began to falter. The new people realized something was wrong, for when the Great Symphony began to falter, their song was also weakened. They thought that by controlling the melodies and notes of the stream, perhaps they could strengthen their song and keep it safe from the rhythms of the earth. The more they tried to control and the more melodies they tried to change to fit their song, the more the rhythms disrupted their song. And it got worse and worse and worse.

I cannot tell you the ending to this story, because it hasn't yet happened. A great palmist could probably read the future of this story in the hand of each of us. The new people could learn the harmony of the Great Symphony and learn to play their melody within its stanzas. Or they could continue to weaken the Great Symphony in an effort to save the song of their grandparents. Whichever direction the new people take, one thing is certain: The Great Symphony will continue in the end, with or without the melody of the new people. And if it continues without the melody of the new people, another thing is certain: The Great Symphony will not be as full, or as complete, for the melody of man is as much a part of the Great Symphony as the seed pearls of mist.

I once had a student in a workshop who was passionate about the fact that when we die, all of our body is taken up into the life forces of other living things. She was consternated by the problem of making a story out of this fact. I asked her to think of a personal anecdote or an anecdote from a friend or someone she knew that seemed related to her "passionate fact." She told a story about a man who had been buried under a tree, maybe a hundred years ago, in her small Massachusetts town. For some reason, the townspeople had to dig up this grave. When they did so, they found that the man's body had completely disappeared inside the remnants of the coffin box, but they could see where he had laid because the root system of the neighboring tree had completely nourished itself from his body and taken on his form, from head to toe. To me, this story was perfect. Perhaps there could be a clever way to set up the beginning of the story so that it supported the full power of the culminating image, but the image itself couldn't be more powerful. It is a perfect image and archetype for the information she wanted to communicate.

The Weed Archetype

The "weed" archetype is a story that reverses the public's preconception of something that has always been viewed as a nuisance or a "weed." Ironically, many of these perceived weed species, such as coyotes and rattlesnakes, are native to the North American continent. Often I have heard this weed analogy made in public hearings by proponents of exterminating the so-called weed that stands in the way of their desired land use. Frequently, the slaughter of coyotes has been justified in the context of weeding your garden. Biologically, this "weeding" exacerbates the nuisance by destroying the coyotes' pack structures, which, in turn, forces them to survive on easy-to-kill domestic livestock. Predators, as a group, have been historically considered weeds by the dominant culture in our country until the work of Aldo Leopold (who was head of a predator eradication program when he had his "awakening"). Yet, despite Leopold's work and the work of numerous scientists since Leopold, the weed argument still rears its ugly head. The world is full of these weed stories.

- Taxol is a promising new anticancer drug derived from the bark of the yew tree, which was almost eradicated as a weed in the monoculture management of Northwest forests.
- Coyotes provide a necessary balance to the ground squirrel population. Undisturbed in the wild, they mate for life and prefer to hunt in packs. When their pack structure has been destroyed by indiscriminate killing, they prey on animals that are easier to catch, such as livestock, and produce larger litters.
- Snake venom has been used as a medication for lowering cholesterol. (Agnes Vanderburg, a Flathead friend of mine, once told me a story in which Rattlesnake saved the people from an all-consuming skeleton-head monster by taking out its fangs and putting them in a soup that was fed to the monster.)
- Spotted owls eat a small rodent called a vole, who in turn loves to eat a certain truffle fungus, which, in turn, is a necessary aide to the germination and growth of Douglas fir trees. Through their digestion and excretion, spotted owls help spread this fungus, which is so necessary for the growth of Northwest forests.

From a purely literary point of view, weed stories are particularly strong because they contain the element of surprise. People are always surprised to find something beneficial in that which they loath or fear. Weed stories have the potential to become hero stories—a kind of "Ugly Duckling" that triumphs as the underdog and in the end is recognized for its virtues.

SCIENTIFIC METHOD MYSTERY STORY

The scientific method in literary terms is a mystery. One can reveal an entire body of scientific information through the course of trying to solve a mystery. This must be the same for an effective scientific story or scientific information. Presented in a slide show, a scientific mystery begins with a big question, such as, "Why are species of salmon disappearing?" Often, such a question generates subsequent questions, such as "When is a stream healthy?" These series of questions or problems-to-be-solved make up the essential structure of the story. With an outline of these prepared in advance of a public presentation, the interpreter should be able to avoid that all-too-common ailment of interpreters: wanting to give too much information. In a mystery and in any good presentation, information never presents itself without being needed or without the detective asking a question first. In stories of discovery, questions are the "hook" that keeps the audience interested. They are the story's muscle. They give the story shape and keep it moving forward. Also, while being engaged in the search, the audience will gain an appreciation for the scientific process—that arduous journey toward knowledge that modern folks often take for granted.

INTRODUCE A SCIENTIFIC TALK OR SLIDE SHOW WITH A MYTH

This form is described in chapter 5 when I spoke about a performance I gave for the opening of the Newberry Volcanic Monument. I performed three creation myths in which a churning of forces, uplift and the creative forces of fire and ice were all part of the archetypal dramas. U.S. Forest Service geologist Larry Chitwood followed my performance by saying, "Ah—yes, well, it's kind of like Susan just said ... ." He continued his part of the program by telling the same stories in specific scientific terms. Then, he was followed by the forest archaeologist who gave the earliest human history stories for the area. Today, I try to weave some slice of science story in between every mythic performance I give in order to further establish all the ways one can speak and hear truth. Michael Caduto and Joseph Bruchac's *Keepers of the Earth*® series of books (Fulcrum Publishing) are good sources for this way of working with story. Always take care not to expect a myth to speak informationally. As this way of working with story has gained popularity in the past few years, I have met several interpretive and education professionals who expect myths to have immediate didactic effect. One must remember that a story is not a thing: It does not enforce a result like a law; it does not control a herd like a fence. It works over time on the imagination of the listener, and being an activity of imagination, its primary power is image. Therefore, look to the images of a story for a connecting thread to your information objective. Here is an example from my performance *Secrets from The Dark Forest: Tree Stories.* Toward the end of the Nordic Creation Myth, the great world tree, Ygdrasil, is created and described. A great amount of that description is devoted to its root system and the life that thrives in relation to it.

YGDRASIL

Down into the dark earth, Ygdrasil sends her roots. There are three roots. One stretches into the realm of Erda, the Goddess of Life, from which all things are nourished and blossom. Fairies sprinkle dew from her sweet waters every morning upon the tree to keep its leaves green.

To the other side, the tree bears a more painful burden than mortals can conceive. Into Nifel-heim, the root stretches and takes up waters from its ice cold fountain. There lives the corpse-eating dragon, Nidhog, who is gnawing constantly on the life force of the tree. Age rots the root and a multitude of creatures gnaw at and twist through its tender fibers. For ne're was there good to which evil came not—nor growth without decay.

In the center, a root, white as light, stretches down, down into the well of all memory and the home of Mimer—the God of Memory. Deep in this dark rooty realm, Mimer keeps company with a multitude of little black men who regenerate the world. They are busy, busy, busy, always making a special mead. It is said that any mere mortal who passes through the forest and gathers into their senses the sweet smell of this mead as it sifts up through the soil ... that they will become so intoxicated with the divine ... that words will fall forth from them as if from the mouth of the first creator ... and poetry is born.

Up and down the tree runs Ratatosk, the squirrel, who is busy, busy, too. Carrying messages, gossip and news from the realms above to those far below and back again and again ... .

Following this myth, I tell this brief anecdote:

Once, I went out into the middle of an old-growth ponderosa pine forest with a group of other people to hear the famous forest ecologist, Jerry Franklin, speak about old-growth forest ecosystems. Jerry was chosen to be part of the notorious "gang of four" ... four ecologists who were asked by President Bill Clinton to help find a viable solution to the old-growth issue.

From our seats on the ground, he towered over us like the big ponderosas that made up his backdrop. He began with a history of what was originally believed in forest management and how that knowledge was changed by the work of graduate students, professors and field managers. At one moment, he broke into an absolute passion about one such changed misconception—that we can grow trees of old-growth magnitude by artificially fertilizing the soil. His hands and arms started to gesture like the great swaying, solar-collecting, sugar-producing bunches of pine needles in the branches above and around us. "Everyone keeps talking about the soil," he was picking up wind, "talking about what to put in the soil ... what the soil can do for the trees. It's not what the soil can do for the trees—it's what the trees can do for the soil! By God! These boughs produce amazing amounts of sugar that they send down into that whole other world below the surface and supply the lives of millions of microorganisms ... which support the tree in ways we still don't fully understand. It's like the roots were being filled with white light."

For me, the memorable archetypal image that connects both the myth and scientific story is the "white light" of energy that fills the roots. It is uncanny that both Jerry and the myth use this exact term "white light" unbeknownst of each other. It is precisely this cross-association of image that reveals the archetypal core of both the scientific and mythic truth in a story. This image of "white light" running throughout the tree perfectly communicates the concepts of the tree as both the translator of awesome amounts of energy and as a life source to an entire ecosystem.

SCIENCE LACED WITH MYTH

For this form, weave the telling of one or more myths throughout a discourse on a scientific subject. In this excerpt from his book, *Gaia: A New Look at Life on Earth* (1979), scientist James Lovelock spills a bit of myth into his discussion of how life began on earth.

If we can imagine a planet made of nothing but the component parts of watches, we may reasonably assume that in the fullness of time—perhaps 1,000 million years—gravitational forces and the restless motion of the wind would assemble at least one working watch. Life on earth probably started in a similar manner. The countless number and variety of random encounters between individual molecular components of life may have eventually resulted in a chance association of parts which together could perform a life-like task, such as gathering sunlight and using its energy to contrive some further action which would otherwise have been impossible or forbidden by the laws of physics. [The ancient Greek myth of Prometheus stealing fire from heaven and the biblical story of Adam and Eve tasting the forbidden fruit may have far deeper roots in our ancestral history than we realize.]

In essence, photosynthesis is the Prometheus story of stealing fire from heaven.
From Robert Lawlor's book, *Sacred Geometry: Philosophy and Practice* (1982), comes another description of creation with reference to Egyptian myth.

In ancient Egypt (Egyptian myth) the primordial vibrational field is called Nun, the primal ocean. It is the One imaged as undifferentiated cosmic substance, the source of all creation. Submerged within this primal ocean is Atum, the creator, who must first distinguish himself from Nun in order for creation to begin. Atum is masculine, and analogous to Chit (consciousness-force) of the Indian myth. Atum is pictured in a state of total self-absorbed bliss. Some versions of the myth say that Atum is masturbating. His blissful self-contemplation provokes his ejaculation, and this ejaculation catches in his throat, causing him to cough his own seed out of his mouth. He coughed and spit out Shu and Tefnut, who, together with himself, form the first triad of the nine great Neteru or principles of creation ... .

... The hieroglyphic sign for the (creator's) mouth ... and the mathematical notation for denominator (the divider) ... is the same sign used to write the name of the supreme being, Atum ... .

Today, in the field theory of modern astrophysics, the universe is conceived as an integral, incomprehensibly vast vibrating field of ionized, pregaseous plasma, an image not unlike that of the Nun or cosmic ocean of the Egyptian myth ... . Within this field gravitational influences are triggered, which cause a warp and densification into nodal patterns. The disequilibrium and turbulence caused by the newly formed galactic mass-centers under the forces of contraction release compound ripples causing violent abrupt changes in the pressure and density of the whole cosmic plasma. These are referred to as galactic "sonic booms," sonic because indeed the propagation of any sound is simply the rapid oscillatory pressure-density change in any medium. These whirling sonic shocks create a spin in the entire galactic cloud and within the inner regions set up by this spin the stars are born. This clearly restates the ancient image of universal creation through sound waves or the word of God; science reaffirms that visible stars and galaxies are spiral blast patterns, residual imprints of standing shock waves from the thundering voice of the universe.

SCIENCE LACED WITH HISTORY/
HISTORY LACED WITH SCIENCE

Weave the telling of pertinent history throughout the telling of a scientific discovery you intend to interpret—or vice versa. This sets the whole process of scientific discovery into a chronology of successes and foibles impacted by both the limitations and advances of the politics, sociology and technology of a historic period. Or, in reverse, one could show how scientific discovery impacted changes in political or sociological trends. This story structure creates human interest by showing relationship between the scientific and the human.

The following is a sample from James Burke's book, *Connections* (1978). In each chapter, the author begins by describing an invention (such as the horse stirrup) and through a chronology of this invention's influence upon society, politics or other new inventions, he shows how one invention was ultimately related to some modern invention (such as the light bulb). Since it is not necessary to repeat Mr. Burke's entire text here, I relay excerpts that demonstrate how he keeps "the hook" or the muscle alive in his telling of these fantastic history/technology sagas.

[speaking about nuclear fission and fusion] Few breakthroughs in military technology have had similar potential for altering the society that first uses them. One such breakthrough occurred in Europe just over a thousand years ago. On that occasion the device was also small, both sides possessed it, one side used it first, and the results of its use were radical and far-reaching. Indeed, had the device not been used this book might well have been written in a different language ... . The first effect of the device was to change the government of England. [tells about the battle of Hastings]

The battle of Hastings was recorded eleven years later on the Bayeux Tapestry. To modern eyes it is a crude, childish work. It reveals the clues to the device that William knew how to use and Harold did not—and that ultimately gave England to the Normans. The device itself is hard to see on the tapestry, but its presence is apparent from something else that can only be there because of it: the kite-shaped shield carried by a rider whose right arm is occupied holding a lance, and who is therefore too busy to protect his vulnerable left leg. The fact that the shield is long enough to protect the entire length of the body reveals the extent to which the right arm is busy, and the only thing that would keep it so busy is a lance. And the lance is there only because of the device in question: the stirrup. It was William's use of the stirrup to build a shock-troop of cavalry that gave him the ability to ride down the Saxons once they were on level ground ... .

INVENT A STORY

A perfect example of an invented story that weaves together scientific fact (such as "butterflies smell through the bottom of their feet") and broad scientific concepts (such as biodiversity) is storyteller Jay O'Callahan's *Herman and Margaret.* The story begins in a lonely orchard where the trees have stopped producing fruit. Herman, a worm, disobeys his wise grandfather and ventures up to the surface of the earth. Aboveground, Herman has a near-death encounter with the drying powers of the sun, and then is saved from a bird attack by Margaret, a caterpillar. They build a friendship through the seasons. Then, Margaret needs Herman's help. Herman learns from his grandfather about the changes that caterpillars go through and how he can help Margaret. At first he says to his grandfather, "Oh, what can I do? I'm only a worm." But Herman's grandfather explains why worms are so important and teaches him this song:

> *What we do down here, helps them live up there.*
> *What we chew and how we move,*
> *How we wiggle and how we squiggle ... .*

At one point, the grandfather calls up all the worms from around the world to hum and sing together. Making a world vibration, they help free Margaret from her chrysalis. We hear how the blood slowly enters into her wings and she gains her strength. Now, she begins her important work of pollination and all life begins to return to the once lonely orchard. Like the best of Native American mythology, the teachings in this story are ecological in both the social and scientific senses of the word.

TELL A SCIENTIFIC STORY IN THE LANGUAGE OF MYTH

I place this at the end of my story structure list because I believe it is the most difficult to pull off. Although schoolchildren are frequently asked to perform this task as part of a learning activity, modern myths never seem to have the same power as ancient ones. Perhaps this is because the ancient ones have passed through so many mouths that they have been refined by the touch of thousands of artists. Also, I believe that the original myths were created out of the dreams and visions of shamans or wisdom keepers. The following is my own attempt. I created this story out of some actual dream images and long discussions with Larry Chitwood, a geologist. It was created for a performance at the Lava Lands Volcanic Visitors Center.

LAVA LANDS CREATION

First Man and First Woman stood on the water. There was only water ... water was everywhere. First Man had a ball of rock. He threw it up, up, up into the air and shot it with lightning. The rock exploded with fire and began spinning through the air on fire toward First Woman. First Woman just barely touched it. It was so hot! So hot and bright! She caught it for a moment and pushed it into the water.

Sssssh! Cracking, cooling, they heard it as it sunk deep into the ocean. They wanted to see what had become of it. So they dove down through the depths of the dark sea. They swam down through dark caverns where outcroppings of brightly colored crystals grew ... crystals growing in great spires from the cracked and slow-moving molten rock. Blue and green and yellow, sunlight lemon yellow and deep red were the spires. First Man and First Woman broke off a piece from each colored crystal and carried them up to the surface.

Now, the rock that they had sent to the sea below was expanding, miraculously expanding ... exploding into great mountains of molten rock up about itself and out of the seas. And when the mounds of molten rock met the cool waters, it sent up huge clouds of fine shattered crystal dust.

"Oooooh!" First Man and First Woman were delighted. They took the blue crystals from their pockets, crushed them into a fine dust and blew until all of the crystalline dust was scattered across the skies. And they crushed blue and green crystals together and threw them across the seas. "Just this much," First Woman said. "Then, let's see what happens."

Now, when the clouds were coming up and off the ocean, they carried blue and green in their mists ... and when the mountains sifted the cloud out of the skies, they rained blue-green upon the land ... catching in concentrated clusters in valleys and ravines ... where blue-green began to feed on blue-green in the rock ... and green and blue-greens began to grow on the land.

For a long time ... in the beginning ... the earth wore the color blue-green like a water nymph's thin gauze gown ... like the thin fur fuzz about a newborn colt's nose. "Ah! What a beautiful child." First Man and First Woman stepped back to the distance of the sun ... admiring their creation from afar, but holding her close with their outstretched warmth.

Universal months, years and millennia passed by. Then one day, the earth became too heavy for herself. She began to crack, split and fall under a whole other part of herself. There, under her seemingly cool exterior, she was still harboring this passion, this heat, that was given to her by her parents. She couldn't contain it any longer. Cracking and folding in on herself, she swallowed up grand stretches of her lush blue-green beauty. Mixing up all of the colors together inside herself, she spewed out black glass and angry-edged crusty rock. "Could this be our child?" thought First Man and First Woman. They watched her from afar ... stretching, groaning, cracking ... spouting rock, spouting gas like a young dragon ... yes, her skin and breath now were like a young dragon, a young Tyrannosaurus rex, a young Godzilla ... eyeing the universe with an attitude for opportunity ... trying to brake beyond the limitations of its own form ... like a teenager who has to do some reckless, seemingly senseless act, in order to assert her or his identity. And, like the parents of a teenager, First Man and First Woman watched and waited patiently and kept the reigns of orbital pull loose in their grasp. For deep in their own knowing, they knew that great passion creates great beauty and so they waited.

And, like so many parents of teenagers, this waiting seemed to take millions and millions of years. For First Man and First Woman, it did. They offered help where they could. During the bouts between earth and sea, they crushed up other color combinations of crystals. Like yellow and red, which they threw at the base of ponderosa pine, so it could make that thick orange coat of bark for insulation against earth's fires when the lava flowed. Now the forests of ponderosa could sustain themselves, in parts, through these fires and reseed themselves when earth was at rest. And other trees, too. Jack pine and sequoia began to form their living to suit earth's fits of fire.

And so it began this way ... with one addition, one improvement, made out of another ... with a magnified multitude of crystal mixings over millennia, earth's garment of life became what it is today ... more rich, more intricate, more beautiful than any renaissance queen's gown. In time, earth proved to be every bit the artist, the creator, that her parents are and had hoped she would become.

Now you may wonder why I am telling you this story. And some of you may wonder if it is true. To answer both of these I will say ... see for yourself. Stop running around so much ... look ... listen. When the evening light of the setting sun kisses a field of dried golden grasses, look closely, you will see the red and yellow dust I told you about. If you go, on a full moon night, and sit staring into the rushing water near a falls or come out when the snows hang heavy in the tall pine boughs, look closely ... you might see those same blue-green crystals carried to the earth by the sea so very long ago.

Although making a myth can have its drawbacks, having students invent a myth or fairy tale spontaneously, as in a circle story activity, can be a fantastic way for students to review information that was given in an interpretive or scientific talk. A circle story is an activity in which one member of a group spontaneously begins a story and then passes it on to the next person to continue. Each person may recall different parts of an interpretive talk and re-create it in imagery, mythic symbolism and narrative form. If the original interpretive talk did not put information into picture, the audience now has a chance to.

In working with all of the above story forms, it is important to keep in mind two words: mystery and adventure. In his book, *Sharing Nature with Children* (1979), Joseph Cornell speaks of this as "sharing his personal amazement." Rudolf Steiner, founder of the Waldorf School System, stated that in the years of kindergarten through eighth grade, maintaining a strong sense of wonder is far more important than dissemination of information. The scientist's gift is question. With each question, an adventure begins to unfold—the doors to the secret halls of mystery are opened and we are beckoned to enter. No matter what form of story you work with, it must move with this vitality.

7

LEARNING FROM OUR CONTINENTAL ELDERS: NATIVE AMERICAN MYTHS

Coyote sauntered into my life in 1979 while I was teaching English for a traveling outdoor school. This was the first in a series of "happy accidents" that contributed to my evolution as a storyteller. Coyote initiated my journey with Native American mythology and oral tradition. This journey can best be described as a long series of happy accidents or gifts—not career decisions, as some would offer. Meeting Old Man Coyote has been one of the greatest of these gifts. As a European-American, I am not ashamed of my interest in a story tradition that is not mine by ethnic or racial inheritance. I consider this interest a gift, not a lack of political correctness. Over the years of my involvement with the Native American tradition, I have experienced how these stories create a healing and a balancing in both myself and my audience. Also, my journey with these stories has guided me to a universal "earth wisdom" found in all indigenous mythologies, including that of my own ethnic heritage. In turn, this knowledge has enhanced the depth of my work as a performance artist and interpreter—specifically, in developing my concept of nature archetypes as described in chapter 5.

Out of my own experience, I would encourage others. For those of us who strongly feel the American part of our European-American, African-American, Asian-American or Hispanic-American identity, there is no other story tradition that is more profoundly American than the Native American tradition. These stories, which may be between thirty thousand and forty thousand years old, are the first stories to be born out of the North American continent. Like the indigenous stories of any continent, they were inspired by the plants, animals and landscapes of a very specific place—a place we North Americans all call home. Certainly, they are more profoundly American than Pepsi-Cola and apple pie, although they are not always recognized as such. They pronounce a wisdom of balance and respect that is ecological in both the scientific and moral senses. It is my belief, that if carried out into the world in the proper way, Native stories can weather the trials of cultural translation and effect a sense of balance, healing and respect in all of us. With this intent, this chapter will:

- Illustrate specific aspects of the Native tradition that create balance and respect:
  1. Morality: power of the small and fall of the arrogant
  2. Scientific/spiritual fact in a myth
  3. Fool-trickster-creator-teacher, Coyote
  4. Bawdiness and the sacred
  5. Sanctified time for the story

- Continue the discussion of detrimental cultural bias and censorship.
- Discuss the "telling of Native stories if you are not Native" controversy.

Since Native myths are holistic, meaning they usually integrate several moral truths with spiritual and scientific truths in the same story, it feels harmful to the story and ourselves to dissect them for the purposes of this chapter. Therefore, I will present whole stories, as samples from the tradition, and discuss all aspects that present themselves in each story. The first story is from the Karok of northern California and developed from the research of linguist, William Bright, and random colloquialisms of Native friends.

Coyote Goes to the Sky

Coyote was on his way ... making tracks ... tracks ... tracks ... he made his way down into a beautiful green valley in northern California. There was a village of animal people who were all standing around and looking up at the sky and moaning. It seems that the sky people had come down in the middle of the night and stolen two of their young children and took them back up into the sky world ... and the animal people wanted them back.

Coyote knew just what to do. "That's no problem," he said. "I know what to do. I always know what to do. We'll just make some rope. We'll throw it up to the sky. It will stick to the sky and we'll climb up it and bring them down. Yea!"

"Aoooh!" said Grizzly Bear Woman. "Rope that sticks to the sky? Aoooh." But she went off to make some rope.

And the two Duck Sisters were talking, "Quack, quack ... rope? That sticks to the sky? Quack, quack, quack." But they went off and made some of their duck rope.

And Raccoon Woman, she didn't say anything because she knew she was good with her hands.

Now, Coyote went off, too, to make some of his own rope. The whole time he was working, he was singing to himself about how good his rope was going to be. "Ah, my rope is going to be the best rope ... look at this great rope!"

The whole time he was singing, he never heard the little voice of Xah, Spider Woman. She came next to Coyote and said, "Hey! Coyote! I can make some rope that will stick to the sky!"

But Coyote was so busy singing about his own rope that he never heard her voice.

When the time was right, all of the animal people gathered together. Coyote said, "Let me throw my own rope up first. My rope is the best rope." He threw it up and it went up, up, up ... and then, wwwhip ... thop! It came right down on his head. So, Coyote threw up the Duck's rope. It went up, up, up ... and wwwhip ... thop! And then Grizzly Bear Woman's rope. No one had much hope for her rope. It went up and thop!

Again, Spider Woman came. She was waving all eight of her legs and screamed at the top of her little voice, "Hey! Coyote! I have some rope that will stick to the sky!" But, Coyote was so busy telling everyone what to do that he never heard her.

Finally, Eagle, who sees everything, said, "Hey! Coyote! Why don't you listen to Spider?" "Hump," said Coyote, "I should listen to Spider? Everyone knows that Spider makes her baskets flat. What can you hold in a flat basket, anyway? I don't need to listen to a flat basket maker."

But, after Coyote had tried everyone's rope, Spider's rope was the last. He threw it and it went up, up, up ... and bong! It stuck!

Now, all of the animal people would never have thought that rope hanging in the sky could have been possible if Coyote hadn't imagined it. They climbed up that rope ... way up into the sky world. When they got into the sky world, the sky people were having a great circle dance. Coyote said, "Hey! A dance! I love to dance!" Everyone was dancing in little steps, but Coyote was a fancy dancer. So, he was dancing, "Hey-hey-ho ..." all over.

The other animals found their children and climbed down the rope. The last one called to Coyote, "Hey ... Coyote! We have the children." But Coyote? He was still dancing ..."Hey-ya-ho."

So, the animals went down the rope and took the rope with them.

Coyote was still up in the sky dancing! The sky people went home to their lodges in the sky ... and Coyote was still dancing ... . "Hey-ya- ... . Oh! They've gone home." He walked over to where the rope had been. "Oh, they took the rope. Well, it doesn't look so far down there ... the earth looks so soft and green ... maybe I'll just jump! If I jump, I might break my feet ... I know! I'll jump with my head first. That way I won't break my feet ... I could break my head ... I know! I'll jump with my back first. That way I won't break my feet or my back ... I'll break my back ... I know! I'll jump with my eyes closed. If I can't see, it won't matter!" So, Coyote jumped out of the sky with his eyes closed ... . "AAAAAA!" Thup!

He landed right in the middle of the Nevada desert. A hard place to fall. He was dead ... rubbed out! After a while, he started to smell bad, too. Some of his relatives, the other animal people, came by there and said, "Hey, Old Man Coyote is dead! Good! Let's eat him up."

So, they ate up his flesh ... they ate out his insides (Raven especially loves the insides) ... his fur ... his eyeballs ... his tongue ... and after a while, there was nothing left of Old Man Coyote but his bones. Even the littlest people came by, the insect people, and they ate little holes in his bones.

Then, a great wwwwind came by and caught in those holes and those bones ... began ... to sing ... "Coooy-ooooo-teeeee."

Now, Fox, Coyote's younger brother, heard those bones singing and he followed that song to that place. "Ha! Coyote has been fooling around again!"

Fox jumped over Coyote's bones. He jumped over his bones four times ... four times for each of the four directions and blllit! Coyote came back to life! "Aaaah," he yawned, "I have had a long sleep!" And Coyote went on his way ... making those tracks ... tracks ... tracks... .

MORALITY: POWER OF THE SMALL
AND FALL OF THE ARROGANT

One can find Native myths that address the full range of usual moral issues from thievery to murder. Still, two issues seem overwhelmingly Native American because of the frequency with which they repeat themselves in the stories of various tribes. The first I would call "the importance of not overlooking the power of small beings" and the second, "the fall of the arrogant." They are both connected, of course, as expressions of that age-old problem with the ego. Coyote is the perfect model of the ego, both its positive/creative and negative, self-centered manifestations. In "Coyote Goes to the Sky," the positive ego (Coyote's creative idea about the rope) becomes overly impressed with itself to the point that it forgets how to function as part of a community in which even the smallest creature (Spider) plays an important role. In the story, it is literally a deafness (not hearing Spider) and a blindness ("If I can't see, it won't matter!") that creates Coyote's fall and death. This is the same deaf/blind ego that is so impressed with its ability to harness phenomenal quantities of electricity from hydroelectric dams that it can't see the destruction of salmon fisheries. It is the same ego that is so impressed with the efficiency of modern forestry machinery that it can't hear the voice of the withering, sun-baked mycorrhizae in the soil. Spider's rope is like the lesson of the yew tree. Once it was dismissed and even eradicated as a "weed tree" until it was found that taxol, a promising anticancer drug, could be derived from the yew. Spider's rope and the yew's story are both symbolic of social ecology (all creatures have their purpose) as well as scientific ecology, which tells us that a myriad of miracle solutions are possible in the undiscovered mysteries of natural science.

SCIENTIFIC/SPIRITUAL FACT IN A MYTH

In years of telling this story to thousands of people, no one has ever asked me on what Spider's rope was hanging. This illogic in the story is never questioned because the audience knows that Spider's webbing is sticky and very strong—actually able to carry more weight proportionately to its density than steel. Their imagination is satisfied by the scientific imagery. Distinctive of indigenous mythology, animal, plant, mineral and weather characters usually act out some aspect of their scientifically true selves. They are not anthropomorphized like Henny Penny (a chicken who makes bread) or the Three Little Pigs (who live in houses constructed of straw, sticks or brick). Eagle, for example, hears Spider because "Eagle sees everything." Superior sight is a quality of raptors. Also, in this sequence of the story, Coyote berates Spider for making her baskets flat. "What can you hold in a flat basket?" he complains. This line usually gets a laugh because everyone knows that Spider's web is her basket and that, although it is flat, it can hold a lot. This moment is the second foreshadowing of Spider's role as little hero. First with the sticky, strong rope and then with the flat basket comment, the audience is reminded that Spider has distinctive traits to offer and she is honored for them. Here, woven together in one small story sequence about Spider, we find scientific, ecological, moral/spiritual and sociological truth.

These same truths are revealed again in the final imagery of the story when Coyote is brought back to life. At first, we see an image of nutrient recycling or the food chain as all of the animals pick Coyote's bones. Then come the little beings who play a vital role, the insect people. Because they eat little holes in the bones, the wind is able to catch in those holes and the spirit can call up the reawakening or reincarnation of Coyote. Still, Coyote does not come back without the aid of a "relative," Fox. Invoking the powers of creation (the four directions), Fox helps the reincarnation of Coyote become complete. A listener could derive all kinds of ideas or themes from this sequence.

- We are not alone in this world, but sustained by others. (social)
- Life is never dead forever. It just changes physical form. (spiritual)

- We are part of a creative universe. (spiritual/ecological)
- Little beings play a vital role in life processes. (spiritual/ecological)
- Have a good laugh at yourself, because your ego, like Coyote's, will go out into the world often forgetful of past mistakes. (social/spiritual)

Perhaps there are still others. Like any great literature, the more often one listens to these stories the more new levels of meaning reveal themselves.

One of the great gifts of Native mythology, one that is often misunderstood by non-Natives, is that their stories are not pedantic. There is never a singular moral to the story that is hammered into the audience with a final proclamation. Ancient Native tellers must have understood that pedantic statements are not necessary to the effectiveness of story. Traditionally, a Native person would hear his or her tribe's stories hundreds of times over the course of a lifetime. Upon each listening, another level of truth would unfold itself until the full potential wisdom of the story had permeated the beliefs and behavior of the listener. In this tradition, the story's work on the listener can be likened more to the growth of a tree, taking up little by little as needed, rather than the bombastic demands of modern broadcast media.

Tribute to the power of "little beings" is everywhere in Native myth, although Spider seems like a popular characterization of the concept and makes frequent appearances. In a Wasco (Oregon) story, another such small-voiced character is Frost. He rescues a bride who has been stolen by two bear brothers. The bear brothers have trapped her in a cave and covered the entrance with huge rocks. None of the animals, trying with all of their special skills and strength, can break down the rock wall. Like Spider, Frost has the answer, but his voice is so small that no one can hear him. After the other animals are exhausted, they finally hear him. He blows on the rock. It turns white, cracks and crumbles to the ground. The "power of little beings" lesson dramatically shows itself again and again in a story common to many tribes in which Coyote becomes annoyed by a plant that announces (usually through singing) it is more powerful than Coyote. A classic in this motif is the following story (from my book, *Coyote Stories for Children: Tales from Native America*, 1991). I derived this telling from anthropologist Robert Lowie's work with the Assiniboin.

COYOTE AND THE GRASS PEOPLE

Tracks, tracks, tracks … . That day, Coyote was loping along in the wide-open grasslands of the Great Plains. He was feeling big about himself that day. He had brought the salmon to the Columbia River. He had killed a great monster. So, he was feeling especially big about himself that day. He started to feel SO BIG about himself that he started bragging: "It is a very good thing I am doing. Soon the two-leggeds will be coming and they will say, 'How smart that Coyote is … .'"

All of a sudden ... he heard it! That song! Someone was singing off somewhere ... softly ..."Wwwwww ... we are the strongest people in the world."

"Who is singing that?" asked Coyote. He looked around. No one was there.

He went on ... tracks, tracks ... .

The voices came again. "Wwww ... we are the strongest people in the world."

"Who is singing that?" asked Coyote. No one was there! Coyote put his nose into the grasses and started sniffing around.

The song came again. "We are the strongest people ... ." You see! It was the grasses! Yes! All the grass people were singing softly together. "Wwwww ... we are the strongest people in the world."

"Aaah!" said Coyote. "You grasses? Ha! You think you are stronger than me? No! I, Coyote, am the strongest one in the world, and I'll prove it to you. I'm going to EAT YOU!"

Coyote pulled up a bunch of the grasses and gobbled them down ... "Arr, arr, arr ... arrumm! You see, I have eaten you! That proves that I am more powerful than you!"

But just then ... inside of coyote's stomach ... the grass people began to sing again. They sang, "We are the strongest people in the world, because we will make you fart!"

"Hunh!" said Coyote. "That is nothing for a great chief like me." And he went on his way.

After some time there came a little one ... pooh!

"Hunh!" said Coyote. "So that is your power? That is nothing for a great one like me." And he went on his way.

But after a while there came a bigger one ... pooooh! It actually lifted Coyote off the ground.

"Hunh!" said Coyote. "That is nothing ... nothing for a great chief like me." And he went on his way.

But then, there came a ... POOOOOH! It shot Coyote way up into the air ... and ... WHAM! He hit the ground.

"Oooo!" said Coyote. He had bruises on his rump and legs.

POOOOOOH! There came another one, and it shot Coyote way up into the air ... WHAM! "Oooo!" said Coyote.

Now you see, soon Coyote was blowing himself up and down across the Great Plains ... and he was getting all black and blue. So, once, when he hit the ground, he ran over to a grove of poplar trees. He wrapped one arm around one tree and one arm around another and he held on for his life.

There he was ... POOOH! POOOH! POOOH! ... exploding away.

As he fired away the trees started to pull loose from the earth ... eeh ... eeeh ... eeeeeeeeh ... . But luckily, it finally stopped ... and Coyote went on his way.

But, if you look at poplar trees today, you will see ... they look as if someone tried to pull them out of the ground. They look like that because Old Man Coyote was there, farting in that way.

Tracks, tracks ... tracks, tracks, tracks ... .

Again, it is the small or gentle-voiced creature (the grasses, spider, frost) that has true power. The ego (Coyote) doesn't acknowledge its power or importance until pain is experienced. How clearly we experience this in our eating habits. We will ingest all kinds of nonnutritious foods until our body begins to scream at us. If only we could extend this understanding to the health of our planet. How often people will curse "some bird" or "some dumb fish" that stands in the way of operating their business as they would like. Then comes the pain. As the ranchers and farmers in Aldo Leopold's *A Sand County Almanac* (1977) found out, their fields were overrun with mice once they had exterminated that "dumb coyote."

Coyote: Sacred Fool

In both of these stories, we see Coyote playing the role I call "the sacred fool." A search through the great body of Coyote Stories of various tribes will show that Coyote does everything foolish that human beings do or contemplate doing. By demonstrating this foolishness in the safety of a story, we can laugh at his (our) mistakes and hope we learn from them. Because we enjoy Coyote's foolishness so much, we are willing to hear the stories again and again. How unlike the pedantic admonitions or criticisms of an elder, colleague or friend! Coyote, with all his foolish antics, slips into our imagination, behind the front lines of our ego's guard. He is, therefore, one of the world's most effective teachers. This is why it is essential that one never tell a Coyote Story with an attitude of self-righteousness or announce the moral to the story. This blows the whole show. Coyote is us, and we should enjoy his fool's teachings with compassion and humor.

Actually, it is exactly in the moment of humor that Coyote is doing his best work as teacher and creator of social well-being. He accomplishes exactly what Sigmund Freud meant when he wrote, "Art serves as nothing else can to reconcile men to the personal sacrifices they must make to maintain their civilization." (from Ramsey, *Coyote Was Going There: Indian Literature of the Oregon Country*, 1977) Or as a Navaho colleague and friend, Wilson Hunter, once told me, "Now, I understand why my grandmother told me Coyote Stories. She was teaching me about balance: the potential for creating good and bad that lives in each of us—that we must see this potential in ourselves and hold it in balance for things to go well in the world."

This kind of sacred clown or fool character is common in most cultures and Native American tribes. Although he appears as Coyote in most Native tribes, he also appears as Raven (Northwest coastal tribes), South Wind (along the Oregon coastal tribes), Iktomi the spider (Lakota) and Rabbit (among many Midwest and East Coast tribes). Among the Lakota, this character is referred to as a "heyoka," or contrary. The heyoka does everything the opposite of the way it should be done, in order to make a message clear. The famous Lakota medicine man, Black Elk, once said:

> Twenty days passed, and it was time to perform the dog vision with heyokas and the heyoka ceremony, which seems to be very foolish, but is not so.
>
> Only those who have had visions of the thunder beings of the West can act as heyokas. They have sacred power and they share some of this with all the people, but they do it through funny actions. When a vision comes from the thunder beings of the West, it comes with terror like a thunderstorm; but when the storm of vision has passed, the world is greener and happier, for wherever the truth of vision comes upon the world, it is like a rain. The world, you see, is happier after the terror of the storm.
>
> But in the heyoka ceremony, everything is backward, and it is planned that the people shall be made to feel jolly and happy first, so that it may be easier for the power to come to them. You have noticed that the truth comes into this world with two faces. One is sad with suffering, and the other laughs; but it is the same face laughing or weeping. When people are already in despair, maybe the laughing face is better for them; and when they feel too good and are too sure of being safe, maybe the weeping face is better for them to see. And so I think that is what the heyoka ceremony is for. (Niehardt, *Black Elk Speaks: Being the Life Story of a Holy Man of the Oglala Sioux,* 1972)

To emphasize the sacredness of this clown, I include here a story, "Heyoka Brings Water to Sundance," from my own experience. I tell it in my performance of "Water Stories."

> It was in the fourth year that I attended the Sundance ceremony that I experienced a heyoka ... a contrary ... a sacred fool ... for the first time.
>
> Every year at the Sundance, the leading medicine man let it be known that there were certain things that we should or should not do in order to aid the prayers of the sundancers. That year, we were not to wash ourselves with water.

Already, on the first morning of the four-day ceremony, I, a suburban girl, was feeling the sacrifice. I thought to myself, "If I can just throw a little water on my face." So I brought a bowl over to the kitchen tent, filled it with a little water and threw some on my face. "Hey!" came a voice from along the path. I turned to look at a gentle smiling man coming with friends along the way. "You're not even supposed to wash your face!"

So the days passed. We would go in and out of sweat lodge ceremonies and not wash off the sweat. We would just come out from the lodge and feel the sweat and lightly blowing earth dry on our skin. For the sundancers, inside the sacred ceremonial center of the arbor, things were even harder. They couldn't even drink fresh water for four days. They drank sage tea, which was bitter, and they took no food.

On the fourth day, my friend, Gloria, looked very weak. When the sundancers came out from their shady rest under the arbor and danced in their various formations around the great tree at the center, Gloria looked weakly past the crowds of us who danced and sang in support of the inner circle from our shady place in the surrounding arbor.

On the fourth day, he came—the heyoka dancer, or I should say, the one who had a vision to dance as a heyoka. He braided his hair tightly, while the others all let their hair loose in the wind. He painted one side of his hair royal blue. That side of his face, he painted white and the other half, royal blue. All of the sundancers had bare feet or wore moccasins; he wore white Nikes. The sundancers wore ceremonial dresses or wraps, mostly made of red cloth; the heyoka wrapped his waist in burlap.

The sundancers were all in a formation facing the south when the heyoka came jumping and dancing into the circle. He danced wildly before them with a bowl of fresh water. They danced softly, keeping their eyes and thoughts beyond him. He spilled water out of the bowl before their eyes as he danced between them. Sweet, clear, pure water, it would fly up and hang in the air like a vision of clear glass birds who were taking flight before their eyes and then sink to the dusty, dry skin of mother earth.

By the end of the ceremony, by the time I had to pack up, get in a car and drive back to civilization, I had become quite fond of the dust and the dried sweat on my skin. Slowly, I moved through the air to pack my car, like just another leaf or particle of earth blowing around. This feeling stayed with me even through the hour-long drive down from Mt. Hood, through the barrage of roadside mini-marts and fast-food joints, through the commands and demands of city traffic. When I returned to my home in Portland, I hung around a bit—eventually, I moved toward the shower—slowly—reluctant to wash off this thin film of new skin that had bonded me to that experience—that pocket of ceremony—that island of reverence—that island of earthiness. I went into the bathroom. My first shower in six days. I moved slowly to it, like an initiate entering a ceremony—and then, the first threads of clear, cool water rushed down my face and draped over my head and down my shoulders. My heart sank like an old woman kneeling before the alter. My hands reached up to cradle the cascading flow like some monk holding up his begging bowl. I opened my mouth and received the water like a thousand sacrament wafers made out of melted snowflakes. Like manna from heaven, the water fell to me—like manna from my shower stall.

Another excellent example of a sacred clown appears in Anne Cameron's story "Clown" in her book, *Daughters of Copper Woman* (1981). This story elucidates the role of the clown in a particular Northwest tribe. The clown is an actual person who serves society by dressing or behaving in an exaggerated manner. This display acts as a mirror to the self, causing individuals or the entire society to become aware of some truth to which they were previously blind.

Although the trickster-fool-clown character appears in most cultures, in Native American traditions this character has a particularly profound relationship to the sacred. More than just a model of what not to do, the trickster-fool-clown character serves many functions related to health—both in the spiritual and physical as well as the personal and communal aspects. Coyote, the most frequently occurring heyoka and perhaps the most developed, is often dismissed as a simple buffoon by many in the dominant culture. He is not always appreciated for his profundity or complexity. My friend, Wilson Hunter, described Coyote as a being who is never satisfied with the way things are and feels a need to go outside the circle of social beliefs or accepted truths and try out new things. By doing this, Coyote sometimes gets into trouble and sometimes he discovers something wonderful and brings it back to society. Typical of the fool in many cultures, Coyote is very willing to be vulnerable, that is, screw up, be laughed at or even fall to his death (from which he always recovers) in his process of discovery. In this way, Coyote models the relationship of vulnerability to the creative process. Coyote, as a creator, is clearly evident in stories from the Northwest tribes. In these stories, he is godlike. We often hear the phrase, "Coyote was making the world ready for the coming of the human beings."

In the role of the creator, Coyote exhibits the highest aspects of the ego. The Okanogan story of how "Coyote Gets His Powers" (*Coyote Stories for Children: Tales from Native America,* Strauss, 1991) tells how he receives his godlike powers "to create whatever he can imagine and to come back to life whenever he dies." In stories from the region, one phrase often recurs: "As Coyote began to imagine himself, so he began to change into ... . As Coyote began to imagine the stick of wood, it began to change into ... ." With this fantastic, boundless imagination, Coyote frees salmon from two greedy sisters (Wasco, Columbia River), outwits and destroys many varieties of monsters and imagines the eventual solution of sticky rope in "Coyote Goes to the Sky." Even when Coyote does the wrong thing, as in "Coyote and the Grass People," he still creates something— the appearance of poplar trees.

Not only is Coyote a fool, teacher, god and creator, but he can also be downright cruel or demonic. In a Miwok (northern California) story (see chapter 4), Coyote tries to cheat on his wife. He goes off to the dances without his wife who remains at home with a headache. At the dances, Coyote lusts after another woman. When he takes her out "into the bushes," she changes into his wife. He throws her aside and runs back home to find his wife still sleeping. When he returns to the dances, he soon lusts after another strange woman. They go out "into the bushes" and she changes into his wife, also. This time Coyote beats her to death and then runs home. There is his wife sleeping still. When Coyote goes back to the dances, all of the women look like his wife. In other stories, Coyote rapes his grandmother or daughter, eats his new wife's children or presents himself as a medicine man and eats his patient. More than a laughable buffoon, Coyote is the yin and yang of the universe, the devil-savior, the fool-teacher, the destroyer-creator. Still, his heyoka role is his most endearing and impressive.

Bawdiness and the Sacred

Bawdiness is an essential ingredient of the heyoka's pedagogical power. Yet, it is sometimes misunderstood and censored by people of the dominant culture. "Coyote and the Grass People" is a classic Coyote farting story of which there are many. Farting is usually the result of Coyote's self-serving, arrogant or just thoughtless behavior. It is the graphic and metaphoric consequence of such behavior. Some published translators of the stories have sought to soften this consequence by either changing the stories (Coyote got a tummy ache) or the terminology (Coyote fluffed or passed wind). If a story's consequences do not match a character's behavior in strength or graphic detail, then the story's lessons will not be clear or impressive. One such incident comes to mind. A member of the educational staff at a famous U.S. zoo fell in love with my telling of "Coyote and Spider Woman" (Bear River, northern California, *Coyote Stories for Children: Tales from Native America,* Strauss, 1991) and wanted to use it in one of her programs. In the course of the story, Coyote is helped out of the sky by Spider Woman. She makes a long rope. As Coyote goes down on her rope, he looks up at where the rope is coming out. The story continues: "It was coming right out of the end of Spider's butt! And Spiders have big ones, too! So,

Coyote started to giggle at Spider's butt." Spider becomes furious and pulls Coyote back up into the sky. She tells him that she is trying to help him and that he is not being very nice. Coyote promises not to laugh, but the entire sequence repeats itself two more times until Spider cuts her rope and Coyote falls to his death. The director of the zoo's educational program decided this part was in bad taste, and the story was censored. The staff replaced the words "Spider's butt" with "Spider's abdomen." Bewildered, the staff member later reported to me that "the story just didn't work."

Sexual and violent crimes were virtually nonexistent in traditional Native societies. Sociologists, anthropologists and Native friends of mine have all explained that the storytelling tradition had a lot to do with the psychological health of these societies. As my Lakota friend, Brave Buffalo, explained, "We talk about everything in our stories. You see, it is like a river. If you let the river flow it keeps itself clean. If you dam it up, the water becomes dirty." Once I heard Ron Evans, a traditional Cree storyteller, tell a story about Coyote taking off his penis and giving it to Lynx so that it wouldn't "get in the way" when he danced with the women at their moon dance. Later, Ron said about the story, "I was ten years old when I first heard that story. Everyone was laughing at Coyote. The last person I wanted to be like was Coyote. Nothing taught me more about the right way to be around women than that story." Yet, he told us about the time when he was telling this story to a group of fourth-graders at a public school in Virginia. He was told by a teacher that his story was "a dirty story" and was asked never to return. He said, "I know what your people think is a dirty joke. But these stories are not dirty jokes. They are sacred stories. They are how we learn to be in the world." My advice is don't tell these stories if you feel you will need to "anglicize" (culturally censor) them.

Many parents—including my family doctor—have come to me at performances and reported that "Coyote and the Grass People" is their child's favorite story. What they realize is that not only does the story's consequence fit Coyote's actions, but that speaking about farting with their child, in the context of a story, allows their child to freely laugh and talk about a bodily function that may have been embarrassing for them. In short, the bawdiness of Coyote tales allows a child to embrace the fact that they have a biological body and that their body, for all its smelly and oozing aspects, is natural. While this fact is quite fascinating to youngsters, it can be very uncomfortable and even shocking to some adults in the dominant culture. There have been times when I have felt that a particular audience of children was too repressed to hear one of these stories, especially from a stranger. At other times, I have found that such a story was just what the doctor ordered—especially for audiences of middle-school kids or teenagers who sit from the very commencement of an assembly in an attitude of decidedly deep disbelief that they will hear from me anything more interesting than the usual serious, self-righteous, noble savage, "Hiawathacized" version of Native American story. They never heard a real Coyote Story.

Most published collections of Native American myths don't work because they don't present the "real" stories. The stories have been carefully combed and cleaned of all bawdiness or violent imagery by authors or editorial staff just as "Coyote and Spider Woman" was by the zoo educational director. This is why one must do careful research into all versions of a story. Even my book, *Coyote Stories for Children: Tales from Native America* (1991), was almost published without "Coyote and the Grass People." There was a bit of Coyote luck involved, however. My publisher was afraid that the book would not be reviewed if it included the story. The book's editor was Native American. He chose three of my stories to go into the book and then asked if I had a short, funny one as a fourth story. We were on a three-way conference call with my publisher. Hesitantly, I offered up "Coyote and the Grass People" through the silence of my publisher on the other line. It was the best short, funny one I knew. He listened to the entire story, laughed and said, "Now, that's a real Coyote Story. We have to publish it!"

Luckily, some collections list the original sources of the stories so that you can check their published version with the first anthropological recordings. One such case that illustrates this problem is a published version of the Haida myth "Moldy Forehead" or "Salmon Boy." This is a classic Native myth in which a tribal member comingles with an animal tribe and thereby creates an interrelationship between these particular animal people and the human people. In this case, the "people" are the salmon, a very important people in the Northwest. The comingling occurs when either the protagonist marries one of the animal people (as in the Haida myth "The Woman Who Married a Bear") or the protagonist goes off to live with the animal people and learns their way (as in "Salmon Boy"). These stories usually involve some experience of sacrifice, which establishes the serious nature of the newly created "relative" status and the taking of this relative in the act of hunting or fishing. In "Salmon Boy," a hungry, whining young boy leaves his people during a famine and journeys with the salmon people to their home in the ocean. He learns certain rituals for maintaining the health and plentifulness of the people while he lives among them. When they return to the rivers, during the spring rains, Salmon Boy accompanies them. But he does not realize that he has changed into a salmon. When he sees his mother fishing with the other humans along the shore, he gladly swims up to her. She catches him, clubs him and cuts off his head. When she recognizes him as her son (from a necklace he is wearing), she and the others perform a ceremony to bring him back to life as a human. Yet, he has changed. He is a shaman and does not wish to live among the human beings. He teaches the humans traditions that will ensure the health of the salmon runs and guard against future famines. He returns to live among the salmon and calls the salmon back to the rivers every spring with his drumming. In some published versions of this story, the sacrifice committed by the mother killing her son is changed into a nonsacrifice in which the mother cradles and rocks the son in her arms until he is human again. I prefer the original recorded version, because I find Salmon Boy's sacrifice and his and the salmon tribe's renewal to be authentic images of the relationship between humans and nature. This original image of sacrifice reveals the following themes:

1. We kill things in order to live.
2. The life we take is sacred.
3. The life we take should be respected and not wasted.
4. This life should be experienced and treated as family.
5. With due respect, life is renewed.

Bawdiness and violence in old myths and fairy tales are authentic metaphors for life and serve a purpose, unlike what is found in most television programs.

SANCTIFIED TIME

Every aspect of the Native storytelling tradition concerns itself with the sacred balance and the relationship to one's surroundings. This includes the time and setting in which stories are told. Tellers have to make their own intuitive judgment about which stories are appropriate and when. As described earlier, there are some audiences for which Coyote's bawdiness would be too strong a medicine, and there are some audiences that may require the strongest of Coyote's medicine. This was evident, also, in my story about telling the old English tale, "The Hundredth Dove" in response to the feisty California schoolboy (chapter 4). Attention to the time and setting that is ripe for a particular story extends to all cultures. Yet, the strict attention to appropriate timing by elder Native friends of mine has stimulated my own further contemplation of this matter—far beyond merely following the rules.

For many tribes, the rule is to tell the myths only during the winter months and at night. The start and cutoff times generally follow the weather shift from warm to cold or appearance of first frost and vice versa. I have never heard any explanation for this strict tradition, but as a storyteller of so many years, I have my own explanation. First, setting up a specific time for the stories, no matter what time that might be, creates an atmosphere of ceremony around the stories. This lets the audience know that there is something sacred about the event of receiving the stories. They aren't just entertainment and they aren't just talk.

Second, the stories speak their wisdom in the mysterious language of metaphor and symbol, like our dreams. It makes sense that we hear these stories close to the dream time. In the morning, we are still a bit in the fog. During the day, we are busy with the work at hand. In the late evening or night, we are naturally in an introspective mood, reflecting upon the events of the day and the patterns of our life. We often like to stare into a fire at this time as if the fire were some mirror for reflecting upon ourselves. Stories work on the internal human. Listening to stories is an introspective activity because listeners immediately associate their own experiences with that of the story characters. Therefore, late evening or night is the time when humans can be most receptive to the workings of a story. Late fall and winter are the introspective seasons of the year. In a sense, they are the night or dream time of the whole year. Even tropical regions have introspective seasons as when the rains come. Assessing this introspective time, or when your audience is in what psychologists call a "receptive mode," seems to me to have something to do with quality of light (evening or night by campfire) and also temperature or weather (rainy, snowy).

This tradition of telling stories at certain times of day or year make sense for stories out of other traditions, also. It doesn't feel right, to me, for instance, to tell the Grimm fairy tale "Snow White and Rose Red" at any other time than winter or early spring. The central archetype of the story is the bear. Overall, the story speaks to the theme of hiding, healing, hibernation and rebirth. This is what winter and the transition between winter and spring is about. In most indigenous cultures, the outside world mirrors the inside world of the story and vice versa. When this is done with regard for the seasons, it becomes one more way that the story creates relationship with the natural environment. Among the Modoc (southern Oregon), there are some stories that are told only when a certain wind is blowing across Klamath Lake, because the spirits in these winds are spoken of in the stories. This is sacred time for the Modoc. The point is not to determine whether it is more or less sacred than another tribe's rule or your own personal judgment, but rather to notice what can be learned from the rule about how storytelling works or what effect or atmosphere is created when the rule is invoked. Also, I believe it is better to pay careful attention to traditions. There are many things we do not know about the relationship between indigenous traditions and the environment.

The challenge, then, is what happens when we remove these stories from their landscapes and their sacred times? That is, do we tell them in New Jersey? Do we tell them in summer Park Service programs? Over my years of telling, I have grown conservative on this issue. Audiences of the dominant culture tend to belittle the value of Native sacred story. One can hear this expressed in such common attitudes as: "These myths are clever little stories that primitive people created to explain the universe before we had science." And "Oh, they create such charming myths ... but, they aren't true ... not like Bible stories." I have been invited, upon occasion, to give story performances in half-hour intervals throughout a day, six days a week over the summer months of peak tourist visitation at museums, zoos and theme parks. Scheduling like this tells the audience that the teller is an entertainer and a video player made of flesh and blood. How different this is from the one evening I was invited to Lassen National Park where the park staff provided me with a campfire and a rich starlit setting.

With respect to school programs, I limit them to the winter months and make sure the performance room is darkened and contains the atmosphere of night. I limit the number of programs because my mental/spiritual exhaustion always exceeds that of my physical body. I heed the advice of my Warm Springs friend, Verbeena Green, "Be careful what you tell children. They take it inside of themselves very deeply. Always be in a good mood when you are telling stories, because your spirit goes into the children. Take something (like beads) with you, because you might see one child who is special, and you will want to give him or her a gift."

Robert Preston, a Navaho spokesman of traditional ways, says that one should only tell histories and natural histories in the summer months. Yet, he adds, Coyote Stories can be told in the summer only inside of a sweat lodge. Again, in the sweat lodge we have the atmosphere of dark, enclosed space. A Flathead (Montana) woman once told me that her grandmother used to "sneak" her the stories in the summertime, since she and her siblings were shipped off to Bureau of Indian Affairs (BIA) schools all winter where they were punished for speaking their own language or retaining their culture in any form. Mostly, I tell other stories only in the summer months. In the few exceptions, I insist on a dark, enclosed space for the telling. I make these exceptions only if I feel that I am truly called to serve a greater purpose with the telling. Ultimately, each of us has to make our own judgment, maintain a disciplined restraint, require a specific atmosphere and remember the words of my friend, Verbeena, "What you do is your business. It will always come back to you."

Non-Natives Telling Native Stories

Already we have explored some of the many reasons that non-Natives telling Native stories could be objectionable. Although I could be considered someone with a vested interest in one point of view, I fully embrace both sides of this important controversy. I believe that both points of view have validity and that if we can maintain our interest in all points of the controversy, the stories will be well served. In the following section I will discuss these points of view to the best of my knowledge.

As a contemporary storyteller, I rescript and perform stories from a wide variety of cultures. No one seems to care that I am not Japanese or Afghan and might tell a Japanese or Afghanistan folktale. In fact, people from Japan and parts of the Middle East have often come out of an audience after a performance and expressed pure delight at hearing their culture's tale told. The only cultures for which I have experienced a kind of protectionism have been with Native American and Jewish stories—and although I have never told one, I have heard that the Irish are very guarded about non-Irish people telling their stories, too.

The protectionism about Jewish stories has always been particularly amusing and saddening for me. For although I carry the Waspish appearance of my one-quarter Catholic/Protestant Dutch heritage, I am three-quarters Jewish. And, although I was not raised with the Jewish religion, my mother's mother was Jewish and, therefore, as a sweet old Hassidic Jewish man once told me: "You are 100 percent Jewish!" Often, I have felt discriminated against by Jews who have judged me first by my appearance. Consequently, I have always felt an alliance with the experience of the "half-breed." Once, on public radio, I heard a Mexican writer speak who had won the Nobel Prize for literature. During the interview, it became known that he was not totally Mexican but also had Anglican heritage. When the interviewer asked how he felt about being a "half-breed," he said he was grateful for his mixed heritage, even though it had brought him pain, because it saved him from nationalism. This is how I feel about telling the stories of any culture. I feel it is time that we delight in the particulars of our cultures, that we argue and defend the particulars of our cultures, without indulging in the derisiveness and chauvinism that spills so easily out of nationalism.

I have suffered many years over my involvement with Native American stories and not being Native. I remember once arguing with a European-American friend over this issue until four o'clock in the morning in a motel room—after I had given a particularly poor performance of Native stories. She felt specifically defensive that the right to tell Native stories should only belong to Natives. After arguing, she fell asleep; I lay awake in agony. Finally, I broke down inside and thought to myself, "Why am I so defensive? Why not accept the death of this period of my life—appreciate the wisdom I have gathered from my involvement with these stories and move on?" So, I did. In that moment, I felt this burning pain move across my heart. I felt that I had to say good-bye to Coyote and the other animal people in his stories. In that moment, I fully understood why I tell these stories. It's for the love of these creatures. Nobody else's stories carry the creatures of this continent in them. By leaving the stories, I felt as if I were leaving the very core of what I love about my homeland. Slipping into self-doubt again several months later, I asked a Native friend if she thought I should stop telling Coyote Stories. "Why?" she asked. "Because I'm not Native," I said. "Yeah," she said, "but you're not a coyote either."

Since I began in 1979, every time I decided I had no business working with the Native tradition, I was mysteriously pulled back into it by circumstance. These were what I call "the happy accidents" of my life that interviewers refer to as "career decisions." Finally, I realized that I am a coyote, in the mythic sense, and that I have a life with Coyote. After working with myth, I believe every culture has a special medicine carried in the style with which it expresses truth. If a person is deeply called to work with particular cultural traditions, he or she should embark on the journey. By answering this calling, he or she will find his or her psyche balanced by the work. Artists/interpreters who are truly doing their work are spiritually and psychologically enriched by the process, painful and blissful as it may be. A cultural tradition, be it music, dance or storytelling, does not choose us by color, but by soul.

Still, one should deeply examine one's own attraction to Native culture to make sure this attraction is not superficial or part of some fad. A colleague once told me, "I just don't like Coyote Stories ... ." I commend her, because even though Native American stories are popular with schools (which is her market), she is true to herself. On another occasion, I received an angry letter from a second-grade teacher in Oklahoma who believed that I was "doing a gross disservice to children and to Native culture" by using such words as "fart" and Spider's "butt." According to her, Native people would never be so undignified as to speak about these things. As discussed earlier in this chapter, a great part of Native people's dignity, moral education and grace comes directly from the ease with which they speak and laugh about these "things." Laughing at one's self and speaking about human foibles with humor and story is one of the great strengths of Native wisdom and teaching. This teacher's understanding of Native culture is the result of decades of censorship by the publishing industry and other media efforts from the dominant culture to redefine Natives as noble savages while destroying the very culture it was making noble (cultural colonialism). The "Hiawathacizing" of Native people, as I call it, is equally as racist as negative forms of racism. I have to laugh when I think back to an anthropology professor in college who angrily said to me, "Why are you so interested in Native people? Why do you want to bother them? You will never be able to understand them because you are white," and, then to my first Native teacher, Brave Buffalo, who said to me after I had been asking him a lot of questions, "Why do you ask me so many questions? Can't you see that I'm a human being just like you?" Figuratively speaking, I've had my face slapped more than once by assuming that because someone was Native they also had environmentalist values.

So begins the controversy: to see people as individuals, as individuals from a particular culture and as individuals living in this amazing cultural cooker called modern North America. Keeping all of the above in mind, I still lean toward the conservative on this issue. As much of a universalist as I am, I believe that difference and distinction are to be celebrated. The details of a folktale or myth are like tastes. Each culture has its own version of the pancake. How wonderful are the variations of tastes, textures and uses of each! Would we want to lose those differences? Not in pancakes; not in folk traditions or mythology.

How can we avoid losing these details and bring forth the most authentic work? One, hire a traditional Native teller. Or, two, hire tellers (modern Native or non-Native) who have done their research. I have met Native tellers who were not handed the tradition from an elder, and I have found their stories in published books. Also, I have met non-Native tellers who were trained in the language and tradition by a Native elder. The long process of authentic research—from digging in a variety of original sources, to readings in cultural background, to visiting with people of the culture, to one's own soul searching about the inner truth of the story is described in further detail in chapter 8.

One thing is certain: My live performances, tape-recorded and written renditions of Native myths will never be as authentic as those from a traditional teller raised in the culture. This does not mean they will not be as good as those from a traditional teller or as close to the soul of the story. I have received confirmation of this several times from traditional Natives. Still, a traditional teller has a depth of understanding about the stories and the culture that shows up in the most subtle nuances of their voice, face and general manner. Featuring different tellers, some from the culture and some not, can actually heighten these subtle distinctions and build a rich interpretive experience for the public.

Suggestions for Festival or Interpretive Center Managers

One pitfall that frequently accompanies a manager's desire to be "authentic" or "politically correct" is the assumption that because someone is Native, he or she is also a storyteller. I have seen this assumption made so frequently with Native people that it is obviously a patronizing form of racism. It can be embarrassing for Native people to be expected to know something that (1) may not be of interest to them, or (2) was systematically bleached out of their heritage. Many Native people were stripped of their family life and taken off to be educated in BIA schools where they were severely punished for speaking their own language or exhibiting any aspect of their cultural traditions. The Flathead woman (Montana) who once told me that her grandmother would sneak her stories in the summer after she had come home from a year at a BIA school also told me that her grandmother did this even though it meant she would risk getting a snake bite (breaking with tradition). For this and other reasons, many Native languages are on the verge of extinction, and Natives who have a depth of experience with the story tradition are also rare. Problems that plague Native communities, such as drug and alcohol abuse and the disintegration of traditional parenting practices, were all exacerbated by BIA's acculturation efforts. These problems have disrupted the passing on of storytelling traditions.

Until very recently, the non-Native majority in this country has not viewed Native mythology with more regard than "those cute little stories that primitive people told before they had science." This year, for the first time, a parent from northern Virginia contacted me and wanted me to tell Native stories in her child's school as an antidote for the "horribly self-centered and materialistic behavior that is prevalent among the vast majority of the children in our school." I had to laugh to keep from crying and thought to myself, "Finally, they're starting to get it. Now, who is left to share the real stuff?" Even if they are not storytellers, most Native people can share some aspect of their life they feel is characteristically Native. Such a presentation is authentic to the individual's knowledge and experience. Also, it honors who they are as Natives living in modern-day North America. Managers who want to hire a Native storyteller need to learn to recognize that a storyteller is distinct from being Native. Although people may remember a story from their grandmother, this does not make them a storyteller. Do we expect every Germanic-looking person to give performances of Grimm fairy tales or every African-American person to tell Br'er Rabbit stories in an engaging way? Just as every Welsh person is not a poet or actor and every African person is not a drummer, not every Native person is a storyteller.

Locating a traditional teller can require an extension of patience and sensitivity. Going to a tribal culture committee is a good place to begin inquiring. Sometimes just hanging around almost any place or event on a reservation will turn up a suggestion. Once I went into a trading post type of store on the Flathead Reservation and asked the two older ladies at the counter if they knew of a traditional teller. "No," they said, "there isn't such a person on the reservation." I had a feeling that they just didn't like me asking. I looked at the things in the store and went upstairs into the bead section. There was a young woman about my age, and we talked about making traditional dresses (a side interest of mine). Then, I had a feeling that I should ask her again. She said, "Oh, you should meet my grandma." Her grandma was Agnes, one of the great gifts in my life. Park managers or festival organizers often don't understand or have the amount of patience required to establish a relationship with traditional dancers, storytellers or other practitioners of cultural life. The organizers of the Leavenworth Salmon Festival (Washington) have patiently worked at a relationship with local Natives over several years. In addition to being patient, one can have an easier time encouraging interest from traditional storytellers by doing the following:

- Do not pick the summer months for your storytelling event. Summer is good for other traditional Native activities.
- Ask the teller what kind of an environment he or she would like:
  —indoors or outdoors (without sound distractions)
  —with a microphone or without
  —with a backdrop or without
  —small group or large group
- Ask the teller what time of day would be best.

Remember that storytelling is not an evangelistic art form in Native culture. Don't expect your teller to drive home strong messages about saving the environment. Native elders have watched the dominant culture hurry to use and abuse this earth over the past hundred years. What do they think now that we are in a big hurry to remedy the mess with a few stories? The experience of story works in more subtle ways, and the environmental awareness created by the stories is carried subtly within its ways. Therefore, the storytelling experience requires a more subtle, focused and contained atmosphere in which to show its flowers.

Let's end this chapter with one final story.

God, Too, Lives in Northern New Jersey

For many years now, I have taken Coyote Stories and other tales of the animal people to the schools of New York and northern New Jersey. Like some kind of missionary, I travel now in reverse from the West to the East, bringing Native wisdom to the underprivileged of the upper middle class. Flying in over Newark, I watch over a landscape that was once sacred to a Native people ... once one of the richest wetlands in America at the mouth of the Hudson River ... and is now gray. Grayed by oil refineries. Grayed by overlapping strips of asphalt. Grayed by car exhausts.

When I arrived at that school on that day, the principal seemed bothered to have to deal with me. He led me down into a dungeon of a room that was three times as long as it was wide. He had cafeteria tables put together for a stage. I was supposed to stand on these rickety tables, four feet above the ground in my buckskin dress, screaming out to the kids at the back of the room, telling stories about the sacredness of the earth.

Today, I would not have accepted this situation, but back then, I was still an evangelist. When the kids came in, I bellowed out to all of them, "IT WASN'T LIKE THIS LONG AGO." I spoke to them passionately about how it used to be when the stories were told in the olden days and how the animals were important and that if you had a dream, in which an animal visited you, that animal was trying to share some of its medicine with you. Then, I told the stories.

When it was all over, the kids filed out of the cafeteria and a small pod of children swam up to me through the crowds. You could see they were touched. They asked one question after another. All the while, one little boy stood silently in the back of the group. His eyes were on fire. I interrupted the questions and asked this boy if he had a question. He gathered his voice and said, "I have dreams of animals ... all the time!"

It was then that I realized that God, too, lives in northern New Jersey.

8

Researching a Story with Head and Heart

Once I listened to an impassioned discussion about research at a conference of storytellers. Some of the tellers argued that the authenticity of a story was "the most important thing." They cited gross misrepresentations of cultures by story versions that had been censored or "edited" by publishers. Others argued that one story can have many different versions, and so how can one determine the most authentic version? And what about artistic interpretation? Many agreed that "the most important thing" was to have a good intention, or what storytellers will often call "good heart." They argued that if one has good heart, how can anything be wrong with what a teller is presenting? Penninah Schram, a storyteller specializing in Jewish stories, recalled the years of training and scholarship that a rabbi must undertake before earning the right to speak with authority about the stories of the Torah. She asked the audience of storytellers, righteous about their own points of view, if research couldn't be done with both the head and the heart.

I stand counted in Penninah's camp. First, we must consider that it is impossible to not change a story, somewhat, with one's own artistic interpretation. The Jews call this one's "midrash." Midrash stories are the stories that early rabbis made up to explain gaps in the logic of the Torah stories. There can be several midrash stories for any part of the Torah stories.

Also, stories appear in different versions because they were influenced by changes in the political climate of an era or because the story might have traveled by word of mouth to a neighboring country. This is true of most cultures' stories. The Greek myth, in which Persephone is stolen by Hades, changes by the time it is told by the Romans. In the Roman version Hades rapes Persephone; he doesn't just steal her. Sometimes this change is even more subtle, as in Native American stories that were recorded by Christian missionaries. Many Native American cultures refer to a plurality of divine beings, such as Coyote and South Wind (Oregon coastal tribes), or they refer to the Judeo-Christian concept of

111

God in a pluralistic way, such as "that force which is always shooting up and out in all green things" (northern California tribes). This pluralism was made singular in the term the "Great Spirit" by non-Native writers. Anthropologist Dr. Allen Dundes once reported to me that he had no respect for the storytelling profession because he had met so many who eliminated the finer details of a culture's myths in their efforts to demonstrate the universality of all cultures or because "they wouldn't be accepted in mainstream culture." He cited a case where a minister had "cleaned up" a Native American story and used it in a sermon to demonstrate how Natives believed the same way as Christians. In chapter 7, I cite other censorship problems specific to Native American myths that are not so subtle. Obviously, the truth can get twisted between our desire to interpret and our desire to force a message.

HEAD RESEARCH

Only with much "head" research can a storyteller/interpreter, historian or scientist stay close to the truth. It is out of respect for this depth of research that scientists and other resource professionals often become angered with the shallowness of interpretive presentations. Depth of truth need not be sacrificed due to time constraints or keeping the audience entertained.

How much research is enough? There is never enough. This is especially true when researching Native American mythology. The best sources to begin with are anthropological or linguistic texts that can be found in such academic sources as:

- *The Journal of American Folklore.* It dates back to the last century and is still published today. An excellent source for all cultures.
- *American Folklore Memoirs.* It was published in only eight volumes at the turn of the century.
- *Bureau of American Ethnology* and its index.
- Many universities have linguistic or anthropological publications. Some of note are the Universities of California, Washington, Arizona, Nebraska and Columbia University. Columbia and the University of California Berkeley were the first schools in the United States to support the early efforts of anthropologists.

The *Bureau of American Ethnology* index is especially helpful for referencing articles in its own and other publications. After a while, you can begin to get a feeling for which anthropologists were doing work with which tribe or culture, at what time and where they published their work. Also, you can begin to understand the idiosyncrasies of the anthropologists who were doing the recording at the turn of the century. It is very important to become familiar with the anthropologist as well as with his or her material. Some were staunchly puritanical and did not have a very respectful or compassionate attitude toward the people they were studying. In these texts, the bawdy parts are often written in Latin so as not to be understood by the layperson. Other anthropologists, such as Alfred Kroeber, were much more sensitive. Yet some Natives today insist that his publications don't accurately represent their culture. One can also be helped by the recordings of people who were not professional anthropologists or linguists, but who had a devoted interest and sensibility for Native culture. One can find their work in books in either the anthropology sections of college libraries or in the Native American section in bookstores. Such people include Frank Hamilton Cushing, who traveled with John Wesley Powell, until he was sidetracked by the Zuni who loved him and invited him to live with them; and Jaime De Angulo, who was a literary man with a profound love of indigenous cultures and who wrote profusely in his journals about his experiences with the Pit River Indians of northern California. Finding such people makes cross-referencing worthwhile.

This kind of research needs to be done with other cultural stories, too. All stories have their roots in indigenous cultures, cultures that were reinterpreted by invading cultures. While the invading culture's version of a story might be more interesting to you, knowing the other versions, especially the original, will help inform your own interpretation. Often, I begin by reading everything I can find in a certain subject in children's folklore collections. The stories are usually very simple and watered down, but I can move through them quickly and begin to let story images burrow in my mind. I will find anthropological texts of perhaps Russian or African-American folktales in the adult section of a college library and see what parts of the same stories were changed. This exercise tells me a great deal, for what people fear to show children is often the most powerful parts of a story (and the part that the children are most fascinated by).

The next part of head research is to read about the religious traditions, games and social mores of the culture from which the story comes. This knowledge can help avoid cultural bias and misinterpretations of the story's images and symbols. For example, once I was working with a Blackfoot myth in which a spirit woman standing on a boulder changes herself into a large hoop inspiring thousands of buffalo to come charging toward her. Then, she changes back into a woman and opens a bag. Out come ten little men who start shooting the buffalo, and she has plenty of meat. Naively, I assumed that the hoop represented some cycle of life. When I researched further, I discovered that the Blackfoot had a hoop game that was a sport for developing the mental discipline of young buffalo hunters. Likewise, if I am working on a story in which a particular plant, animal, geological process or meteorological phenomenon is an important character, I read about its science. This research of the story's "scientific culture" may help me develop the character or the story's logic.

Once a certain familiarity with the story and its culture is developed, the interpreter needs to take the next step: Visit the natives. The Natives are the folks who have real-life experience with the subject. They may be a Native American elder or medicine person, a Scandinavian grandmother, a pack of wolves held in captivity for educational purposes or a college professor whose specialty is forest ecology. These are the people and creatures who can answer your questions and can straighten out misconceptions that may have fallen into the books you've used for head research.

It is also important to remember that not all Natives have the same depth of knowledge about their culture, and they may disagree on what constitutes "truth." For example, once while researching Hassidic stories I visited a Hassidic community in Brooklyn, New York. I was passed from one person to the next, until finally, I met the bookseller. He knew about the stories and their interpretations in print. Likewise, some Native Americans have already absorbed the influences of Christian missionaries into their cultural practices and beliefs. Archie Phinney, a Nez Perce anthropology student at Columbia University, collected his grandmother's Coyote Stories and published them in 1936. A Nez Perce friend of mine told me that they were a cleaned-up version because he was one of those "mission Indians." Sometimes Natives edit or censor themselves because they don't trust that you, as the outsider, will fully understand. Once Alfred Kroeber noticed that a woman informant, whom he visited frequently, would start speaking in her own language whenever Dr. Kroeber's wife was present. When asked why she did this, she replied, "Oh, I know your white women aren't able to hear our stories." Likewise, I imagine that the first few times I enter an enclosure with a pack of wolves, they won't act like their natural selves.

Heart Research

The "heart" part of research starts when you are listening to everything that is happening while you are doing your head research. For example:

- A friend says something on the phone that makes you think differently about the story you are researching.
- A phrase or a special way a Native says something seems more true to the culture than the way it is said in a book.
- You have a personal reaction to a version of a story or something a Native says to you. This reaction helps you to see something about yourself that you could not see before.
- You begin to notice similarities between images or events in your story and a story from another culture, a dream or some piece of scientific or historic information.

- You do not shy away from or change a part of a story that annoys you. Instead you investigate your annoyance (why Snow White is so stupid, for instance).
- You contemplate a negative response that an audience member gives you when you tell the story for the first time.
- You let a personal incident or a memory remind you of why you love this story so much.

Mapping, as described in chapter 3, is a head way of opening up heart reactions to your story. It gives you a disciplined practice through which heart reactions can surface. Here is an example of how mapping helped me to create a full story out of a single source text and no chance of visiting with the Natives.

The story, "Sea Dances in the Trees," is part of my performance, *Secrets from the Dark Forest: Tree Myth and True Stories* collection. Actually, I found several versions of this story in two collections by John Bierhorst, *The Mythology of Mexico and Central America* (1990) and *The Mythology of South America* (1988). It is a story that occurs in different versions among several tribes throughout Central and South America, but I did not locate different versions of the Cabecar and Bribri tribes' tellings. Still, I felt relatively secure with Bierhorst's published version, because I know his scholarship from past research. First, here is Bierhorst's version. The information in square brackets is what an outsider needs for following the story more easily. It is helpful to read an original text without the language in brackets, because sometimes one can hear more of the rhythm in the original telling language.

THE TREE AND THE FLOOD

In the beginning, there was only a large rock and no earth. Sibu [the creator] wanted earth so there could be people. He sent a beautiful woman named Sea to tell Thunder that he wanted to consult with him [about making the world].

Thunder refused to leave, so Sibu continued to send Sea to persuade him. When Sea became pregnant, Thunder decided to go. Sibu lent him his staff for the trip [sending Sea to bring it to him], but Thunder would not accept it and said to Sea, "You brought this for me [now use it yourself for the return trip], but don't leave it alone. Take care of it."

In the middle of the trip, Sea said to herself, "I don't understand why I can't leave this club alone. I shall try it and see what happens."

[Later] when she returned [to look for it], the staff had disappeared. She looked everywhere but couldn't find it. While she was searching, a snake bit her and she died.

Sibu arranged her in a burial package, but she began to swell. He put a frog on top to hold the package down [to keep it from rising into the air]. The frog grew hungry and jumped to catch an insect he saw passing. Sea popped into the air and became a tree. Her beautiful hair was changed into leaves, and in [the leaves] the parrot, the macaw and all the [other birds] made their nests.

The tree pushed and pushed upward, piercing the sky, which was Sibu's house. He became furious and said, "Listen! What a racket that tree makes forcing its way upward. It won't be long before it will break the air."

So Sibu sent two birds, tijerita [a flycatcher, Tyrannidae family, or the frigate bird, Fregatidae family] and pajarillo de agua [a grebe, Colymbidae family], to grab the top of the tree and to make a large circle in space. When the two ends met, the tree fell and was converted into water. The nests of the parrot and the macaw were changed into turtles. The leaves became crabs. [In this way the sea was created, and the surf began to pound.] But the Cabecar know that the noise heard on the shore is the noise made by the wind when it blew through the leaves, which were made from the hair of the beautiful woman, the Sea.

From mapping the story, I noticed several patterns:

1. Sea (or water) is an invisible creative force. Although Sibu is the creator and Thunder is a helper, Sea gets some things moving without which the world would not be complete. For instance:

   • She seduces the cooperation and attention of Thunder.
   • She questions set rules and breaks taboos.
   • She changes forms.
   • She provides a life support for other creatures, both as the tree and as a body of water.
   • She is a disturbance to Sibu, which in turn provokes him to take destructive/creative action.

2. Sea is not the only character to be out of the creator's control. Frog also does not stay where Sibu wants him. Is there a relationship between the froglike creatures of the world and the feminine?

3. The world is not complete at the beginning of the story. (Sibu wants to solicit Thunder's help about making the world.) It is completed by the presence of the sea (water) at the end of the story.

4. Why does Sibu choose Thunder for a consultant? What does Thunder have to do with creating water?

5. Since Sea becomes pregnant by Thunder and the sea bursts forth from her (as a tree) like a birthing, is there a relationship between large bodies of water, trees and weather patterns?

From looking at these patterns, I began to see this story as a model of the cyclical relationship between weather patterns and the existence of a rain forest. Also, I saw it as a dance between both the feminine and masculine creative principles in nature. Mapping these patterns helped me to discover the internal structure of the story, which points to the story's meaning—as Robert Frost told us "the figure a poem makes." From these structures, I was inspired to find my own language to fill out the language of the original text and make a story that would communicate to a modern audience outside of the original culture. Here is my version:

SEA DANCES IN THE TREES

In the long ago times, Sibu was creating the world! Ha! Ha!
Sibu was making all manner of mountains ... and valleys! Ha!
Sibu was creating all kinds of creeping and crawling creatures!
Ha! Sibu was happy!

But, something was missing and Sibu couldn't figure it out.

So, Sibu called for his friend, Thunder.
"THUNDERRRRRR!"
But, Thunder was busy enjoying himself ...
dancing across the sky ... "Kkkkkrrrrrruuumm!"
"Kkkkkkrrrrrruuuumm!" He would be here one moment and gone
the next.

Sibu became impatient.
He called again, "THUNDERRRRR!"
But, Thunder was having too good a time and he paid no attention to
Sibu.

So, Sibu decided that he had to create something ...
something so beautiful ... so exquisite ... so sensuous ...
So that he could catch Thunder's attention.
It had to be something so beautiful ... so seductive ... so sweet.

And so ... he created woman.

He called her Sea
and she was so beautiful ... so exquisite ... so sensuous
that when Thunder first caught sight of her,
"Kkkrrumm" he was right there and she became full with Thunder's child.

Now that Thunder had a wife, he thought he had better make a home
and settle down. Sibu was so happy that he made a walking stick for
Thunder, as a gift. He gave the stick to Sea and told her, "Give this to
your husband and mind you, don't leave it anywhere along the way."

Sea journeyed home to her husband ... going over mountains and valleys ... and more mountains and valleys ... until she came to their home.
When she gave the walking stick to Thunder, he was furious.
"What?" he stormed, "Does he think I have become an old man? Thunder doesn't need a walking stick to get around. Take it back to him! And mind you, don't leave it anywhere along the way."

So, again Sea journeyed over mountains and valleys ... and more mountains and then, she wondered, "Why is it that I have to always take this to that man and that to this man? And I wonder, why is it that I can't just leave this stick here? I shall try it and see what happens." And so, she did.

Oh, how the world is changed when a woman begins to wonder!
For the next time Sea came through that valley, a snake was there and bit her and she died.

Sibu and Thunder were so sad.
They wrapped her in a burial bundle,
but something inside of her was still alive!
The bundle began to bulge and balloon and bounce just a bit off the ground. Sibu said, "Hey, what is this?"
He grabbed a frog near by, put him on the bundle and said,
"Stay here in this place and hold this bundle down!"
But oh, how the world has been changed by creatures who can't stay in one place! The first fly that flew by caught the frog's eye and ... he was gone!

Now, the bundle began to bulge and balloon and bounce just a bit before it burst open and a magnificent tree sprouted forth.
This woman who had once been called Sea was now a spectacular tree!
As the tree climbed the sky, its branches stretched in every direction.
Birds of every color ... birds of every feather came to this tree to rest and make their nests.
And such a cacophony of calls echoed between the leaves,
that Sibu screamed, "What is all that racket down there?"

When he saw the tree, he called for his two favorite birds,
Tijerita, the flycatcher and pajarillo de agua, the grebe.
They flew to the top of the great tree and pulled it down, down, down, down, down ... until its belly burst open.
All the waters of the world flowed forth from the belly of this tree and filled in the lands between the mountains with vast oceans, rivers and seas.

The breaking limbs of this great tree slithered away into the water as
snakes or fish ...
The nests of parrot and macaw fell out into the waters ...
and paddled away as turtles ...
The falling leaves were tickled and chased by the wind until
they changed into a thousand crabs skittering along the sandy shores ...
And the sound of that moment ...
the sound of the wind and that huge crashing tree ...
was swallowed forever in the body of that beautiful woman ...
we now call Sea.

And sometimes Thunder comes for her ...
he calls across her waters and she reaches for him in the ocean breeze.
Then, she gathers herself together and joins him.
You can see them dancing together ... there in the mists of the forest trees.

This process of head and heart research can take years and then, still, some
new information may fly in your window one day. This is the path of a master's
training. There is no use becoming impatient with the process. Although it can
take years to refine a story, the depth of your knowledge will be noticed by your
audience even if you have only a few minutes to tell it to them. Also, if you are
worried about being prepared for this season's interpretive talks scheduled to begin in a few weeks, worry no more. Telling a story to small audiences is something
you must begin doing as soon as you feel you have some understanding of it. As
awkward as it may feel, telling a story can help you to see where you need to do
more research. It is part of your learning process and your heart research.

9

Entering the Oral Tradition: Practical Practice Techniques

There is no way to avoid the discomfort of getting started. Sometimes it's the threat of a scheduled, advertised, upcoming program. Sometimes it's the fury at a wrongdoing that gets the creative juices flowing. Sometimes it has to be sheer will and discipline that pole-vaults us into the process. You should feel assured that once you make your first pole vaults, you will feel the rewards. The reward comes not as money or applause, but in the form of the story fairies. They see us laboring so awkwardly with a story that they take pity on us and send us inspirations in the way of audience reactions, a related comment on the radio news, a phone call from a friend in which a subject related to our story comes up in conversation, a voice out of an early morning dream or a flash of inspiration while taking a shower. Little by little, the story fairies help us to live into the story, and it is exciting. Like a child in the womb, we feel the story kick and turn—we feel its life before it is fully ready to be born into the world. Actually, this early part of the story's development is, for me, the most exciting. It is full of the most growth and self-discovery.

Here is how Garrison Keillor describes the process:

> I would say that the essential element in storytelling is the passion to tell a story that will get you through that struggle of finding out how to tell it. If you don't have that passion to tell a story, you will settle for telling it not very well, which is almost worse than not telling it at all. But, if you have the passion to tell a story, it becomes a wonderful problem in your life—a wonderful problem like being in love. It becomes an irritation, a splendid misery, that might get some work out of a person who will do his little part in adding to the world's knowledge, in adding to the life of the world. (from an interview with Garrison Keillor)

MAPPING IMAGES

Mapping shows its face here again, because the story will keep changing during the early process of practicing the story. Mapping, as described in chapter 8, is just as much a part of research as it is an aid to getting started. Often after an initial map, I will begin to hear pieces of the story try to tell themselves. These are those little voices of the story fairies who come to you in the shower, in an early morning dream or just as you doze off at night. WRITE THEM DOWN IMMEDIATELY when they occur! In my own process, these little pieces of language become some of the first islands of the story. Since the strong images of the stories are the rock on which these islands flourish, I guess we could call these early pieces of language the fruit trees on the islands. Like some tropical bird, I tell a new story by flying from island (image) to island (image) savoring the taste of these various fruits of language along the way.

LITTLE ISLANDS OF LANGUAGE

Sometimes I write these little islands of language into a rough script. Mostly, I begin a story's development with ad-libbing, and a script evolves from that. However, when I first produce a rough script, I pay attention to where I feel the story has to move faster or slower or gain or lessen in intensity. I script phrases to move the needed intensity of the story between the image or language islands. For example, in my story, "Good Bob, Bad Bob" (chapter 6), I intensify the story by creating a building repetitive rhythm in the section of the story where I keep trying to impress Bob with the virtues of a tree. I begin each new virtue by repeating, "Bob, a tree is a ... Bob, a tree can ... Bob, a tree is a great ... ." Then, I frame the end of each virtue with the narrative phrase, "Bob said nothing." Every story has a rhythm. Scripting helps you to enunciate that rhythm. Sometimes you can script that rhythm from the beginning and sometimes, while practicing the story, you will find that your scripted rhythm is artificial and you find a better way by ad-libbing or just stumbling upon it. This explains why it is important to try telling a story many different times and in new ways.

CREATING THE ELECTRIC GRANDPARENT

Next, I tell the story into a tape recorder using my map with these little islands of language and image to help me between sections of ad-libbing the story or rough script. Ann Reveta, a storyteller friend, gives a good suggestion. She suggests that we look over the first part of our map, then close our eyes and imagine how we see the story, then turn on the tape recorder and tell just that part into the tape.

Once you have recorded something on tape, you have created your own electric grandparent. Now, you can listen to her or him again and again and again—just like stories were passed down in the olden days. Each time you listen to the story, it will become a little more rooted in your imagination and memory.

GUINEA PIGGING IT

At this point, you must go out and try it on a live audience. Some people will feel more comfortable telling it to a spouse, their own children or even a mirror before taking the story to a more public audience. I prefer a group of opinionated fifth-graders. They will enjoy a story that is geared for a younger or adult audience, and they will be able to give you intelligent feedback. For me, they are the best mirror. With their expectant faces staring at me, I feel that the story rises up in me with more excitement. I become more fully engaged with the story in my desire to serve their anticipation of a good story. I feel that using a glass mirror as one's audience causes my attention to stay with myself and I am not easily able to lose myself in the story. After telling to a fifth-grade class, I ask them the following questions:

- What was the strongest picture you remember from the story?
- Was there anything that you didn't understand in the story?
- Was there a part of the story that you especially liked?
- Was there a part of the story that especially bugged you?

Then I let them take it. In the process of discussion, they will elaborate more fully on these questions. If you repeat this process with several other classes of the same and of different ages, you can observe a pattern of responses that will clue you into the important feedback. Sometimes I have noticed that young girls respond to different imagery than young boys. These observations have supported the development of my ideas about archetypes—nature archetypes as well as archetypes of the feminine and masculine. Also, throughout this process, you will already begin to change the way you are telling the story, and this can change the audience's responses, too. In addition to giving you clues about which parts of your story need more development, the practice of telling a story many times before an audience is one of the best ways to establish the story firmly in your memory.

Outside of practicing one's story for a test public audience, there are several other ways one can work with a story that help find character voices, word choices, language rhythms and the fuller meanings of its archetypes. These can be practiced with a friend.

There are no rules for eye contact. Often, direct eye contact is the perfect punctuation for a moment. At other times, it can distract the audience from their own imagining of the story— acting as a confrontation or an intrusion. Sometimes, the teller's complete absorption in the story is best for the audience. It allows them to feel invited—invited to join the teller in that absorption and in the allure of the story world.

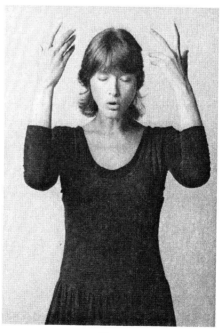

Photos courtesy Jerome Hart

123

Write and Rewrite Your Story as a Poem

Choose different poetic forms such as:

1. Choose three lines from your story to be the poem. These lines could be phrases or whole sentences or two sentences as long as they make a meaningful phrase. Here are some examples from my telling of "Snow White":

Deep in the dark heart of winter, when the snows had just fallen like an angel's blanket slipping from the soft beds of heaven … .

The blood from the huntsman's knife dripped on the earth before he wiped it and put it away.

"It's a nice apple … don't you think … red and sweet."

Other possibilities could be:

"Ah! That I could have a child that was as white as this snow, as red as blood and as black as this ebony wood."

"Over seven hills and seven valleys lives one who is still far fairer than you."

But not even gold would the seven little men take. "Give her to me as a gift, then," said the Prince.

For the purpose of demonstrating how to play with scientific information in this way, I will use the well known story of the water cycle along with the "Snow White" story.

The sun baked the earth all day long and for days and days and days after.

The river water flow line ran far below the stain and cut it had made in the river rocks, years before.

When the rains came, you might have thought that the rocks were singing. Bright green beamed from every plant like a child's smile.

Here is an example of how Robert Frost spoke of the water cycle in his poem, *Spring Pools* (Frost, *The Complete Poems of Robert Frost*, 1965):

These pools that, though in forests, still reflect
The total sky almost without defect,
And like the flowers beside them, chill and shiver,
Will like the flowers beside them soon be gone,

And yet not out by any brook or river,
But up by roots to bring dark foliage on.

The trees that have it in their pent-up buds
To darken nature and be summer woods—
Let them think twice before they use their powers
To blot out and drink up and sweep away
These flowery waters and these watery flowers
From snow that melted only yesterday.

2. With a friend, create a four-line haiku, spontaneously, based on the story. The first person begins by speaking a line. The other must give a line in response. Then, the first person gives a line in response and then, the other. Avoid getting attached to the beauty of each creation and continue to create new haikus. Again, we will play with the well-known fairy tale "Snow White" and a science story of the water cycle to show some examples.

Looking glass, looking glass on the wall ...
Crystalline, like glass, was the snow that fell from the sky.
"Now, don't open the door for anyone!"
The prince couldn't stop looking at her through the glass coffin.

One clear bead of water waited on a blade of grass near the stream.
Down the blade, down the stream, down the river, down to the ocean.
One clear bead of water waited for the morning sun.
Up, up, up into the sky, it travels everywhere!

3. Also, try variations of a four-line haiku using sense experiences from the story.

Snow fell like flakes of starlight.
The queen's lipstick was blood red.
The forest green was a soothing blanket for a frightened heart.
Golden and silver light reflected from the glass coffin.

Clean on the tongue rolls sweet spring water.
The pebbles were red and steel blue below the spring pool.
"Ah! Icy fingers. I should get a cup."
Snow melts against the sun-baked rocks.

4. Try using only dialogue slices from the story.

Although you are fair, 'tis true ...
"Now, mind us, don't speak to any stranger at the door."
"Little Snow White is far fairer than you!"
"Please go away. I was told not to speak to any stranger."

"Pass me a glass of water."

"The fishing used to be good in these parts."

"Fence my stream from cows? It's my stream."

"Because people like their golf and they like their golf courses green."

Notice that while playing with this idea of dialogue slices, you may be discovering what are the most essential pieces of dialogue from your story and the dialogue skeletal structure of your story map.

Speak Your Story as Gossip to a Friend

This is good to do after you have developed a map or rough script for your story. Telling the story as gossip helps you to discover what parts of your script or map are not essential to the flow of the story because gossip usually happens in a quick "let me get right to the meat of the story" style. If you feel uncomfortable doing this, try on a foreign accent. If this is just not for you, try the next idea.

Sing Your Story

Imagine yourself as an old English bard, who traveled from village to village, proclaiming his story in song. Don't worry about the melody, but notice on what words or phrases you like to linger ... creating the rhythm of the melody. This rhythm may suit the speaking of the story, too.

Lie with Your Back to the Floor and Tell the Story in a Complaining Fashion

Take different characters' points of view and tell the story as if you were dissatisfied by the events of the story. Your partner should walk around you and doubt almost everything you say. This doubting should help generate a greater sense that you are not being understood as the victim of the circumstances of the story. It is your partner's job to taunt your sense of righteousness or your belief of having been victimized or just not heard.

You should never consider that a story has reached its full development until you have told it many times over a long period of time. Speaking for myself and other colleagues, a story doesn't fully become itself until I have told it over the period of about two years. Although the story may hold the audience's attention, never lose touch with audience reactions and seek out the responses of those whose opinions you value. The stronger you can be in opening yourself to valuable critique, the more your story and you will grow.

10

VOICE, GESTURE AND MOVEMENT

Voice, gesture and movement are the outward expressions of the internal meaning or archetypes of a story. Scientist/storytellers or historian/storytellers must first search to understand the broadest significance of a particular subject before they can embody that subject in voice, gesture and movement. In a sense, tellers must begin by feeling the subject as a kind of character or being and ask themselves questions such as: How does this thing or being impact the beings around it? How does this thing move in the world and with what speed? In what direction? With what gesture? What special relationships or talents does this being have? After and often during this search for the character, meaning or archetype of the subject, qualities of voice, gesture and movement spontaneously suggest themselves to the speaker. When a speaker listens to these suggestions (and even those during performance), the listener feels the life of the subject in the speaker. This embodiment of the subject is evidence of someone who is truly passionate about it and not merely speaking about its meaning or playacting its relevance. While certain concepts or techniques, such as are described in chapter 3, can influence the way one thinks about one's use of voice or gesture, spontaneous expression is usually more stimulating to a listener's imagination. As speaking artists, storytellers tend to be more successful the more they are willing to dance between preparedness and spontaneous re-creation in each new telling.

Think of yourself as an artist—artist/interpreter or artist/educator—so sayeth chapter 3. But, you might ask the following questions:

- Where do I find inspiration for this artistic expression?
- How do I develop the ability to make artistic choices with regard to voice, gesture and movement?
- What is the value of taking classes and workshops?

This chapter is devoted to answering these three questions. First, I must make clear that the advice in this chapter is based in my experience, and another artist, storyteller, writer, singer or theater artist might answer these questions differently. Since most artists' processes are different, you can find your own inspiration by learning about others'. Even the processes of painters, sculptors, musicians and other artists whose work seems unrelated to storytelling can inform your artist development. One of my favorite statements supporting this idea comes from photographer Ansel Adams, who received professional training on the cello as a young man. He said that his study of the cello was the single most influential element in the development of his work as a photographer.

From where inspiration emerges, what corner, pocket or ant hole, is always a mystery—which, of course, contributes to the agony and joy of any creative process. Playwright Samuel Beckett spent a good portion of his life working in odd jobs so he could find new sources of material and inspiration for his plays. One of the earliest memories of something that influenced my artistic thinking occurred when I was a child. My mother took me to see a performance by the famous mime Marcel Marceau. I remember being amazed by a fluid little hand gesture he made that transformed into a butterfly. I was delighted by the experience and the idea that something so simple could give birth to an entire scene in my imagination.

Tracing back through my development, this same idea—so much coming from so little—struck a chord in me time and time again. For me, this is the essence of storytelling: A teller needs only enough voice and gesture to activate the imagination of listeners and engage their interest. Beyond this, storytelling becomes something else, maybe theater, puppetry and so on. As stated in chapter 3, storytelling is a three-part art, none of which should upstage the others.

GENERAL SOURCES OF INSPIRATION

The following list is a partial chronicle of small events that influenced my work. Notice the sources of the experiences (classes, plays and so on) as well as the concepts derived from the experiences. These may become sources for your own inspiration.

- In a class in creative dramatics that my mother sent me to at age ten, the teacher asked us to draw an animal with only three lines or two lines and a dot. This gave me the idea of how little is needed to create the full experience of something and how important it is to choose those three lines or, as in story or poetry, three details. After making choices of details, you may want to enhance them with qualities of voice or gesture.
- Seeing a play at the Arena Stage in Washington, D.C., when I was a teenager, I became interested in stage design. The play was *Hamlet* and staged with no props, only two stairwells that descended through the floor. The actors ascended and descended these stairs throughout the course of the play as if emerging from and returning to hell. This demonstrated how a setting can create a subtle atmosphere that

reinforces the overall message of the story. I translated this theater idea to storytelling in my version of the Afghan story, "The Nightingale and the Dove" (*The Bird's Tale*, 1985). In this story, an evil queen attempts to destroy a princess and her lover. Each time she has them killed, they transform into some other beautiful aspect of nature. In the end, one of the queen's attempts backfires on her and she dies. Before any of the action of the story commences, I establish a setting that hints at something eternal that survives the ugliness of human nature.

Long ago and far, far away from here on a shore where waves were lapping, lapping, rolling, rounding pebbles, stones for thousands and thousands of years. Once, near that shore ... .

This rhythmic alliteration echoes the waves of rebirths in which the lovers' beauty keeps returning. In the end, two flower bushes grow slowly out of the lovers' grave and little by little form "one strong tree." By contrast, nothing ever grows from the ground where the evil queen is buried.

* Poetry caught my interest early in life and it became my major study in undergraduate school. In particular, the work of Dylan Thomas helped me to see how language can be musical (as described in chapter 3). Thomas' poems often create a mood or speed of action through a barrage of alliterative phrases and juxtaposition of these phrases with silences and staccato syntax rhythms.

The following story is taken from Thomas' "A Child's Christmas in Wales" (*The Collected Stories*, 1938).

All the Christmases roll down toward the two-tongued sea, like a cold and headlong moon bundling down the sky that was our street; and they stop at the rim of the ice-edged, fish-freezing waves, and I plunge my hands in the snow and bring out whatever I can find. In goes my hand into the wool-white, bell-tongued ball of holidays resting at the rim of the carol-singing sea, and out come Mrs. Prothero and the firemen.

It was on the afternoon of the day of Christmas Eve, and I was in Mrs. Prothero's garden, waiting for cats, with her son Jim. It was snowing. It was always snowing at Christmas. December, in my memory, is white as Lapland, though there were no reindeer. But there were cats. Patient, cold and callous, our hands wrapped in socks, we waited to snowball the cats. Sleek and long as jaguars and horrible-whiskered, spitting and snarling, they would slink and sidle over the white back-garden walls ... .

VOICE

Another of Thomas' great contributions is the way he calls our attention to the sounds of words. The words he chooses are made up of sounds that carry the feeling of what he is describing. Words like "ice-edged" create a short, hesitant sound, which is how we feel about icy places. Words like "wool-white, bell-tongued ball" with their "w-w" and "b-b" sounds make the same cold environment seem cozy. Thomas was the first poet who taught me that speaking could sing. For example, when I want to build the anticipation for the entrance of the bear in the Grimm fairy tale "Snow White and Rose Red" and create the buildup to a storm, I use the "w" sound.

One winter—oh, what a storm was brewing. The wind whipped up and around the house—howling and whirling—as the three women gathered around the fire. The fire fought fiercely against the wind as it whisked and whirled and whipped down the chimney.

Robert Frost was another poet, among several, whose work inspired me. As described in chapter 3, he solidified the concept of literature's architecture, or how form creates meaning. Frost can turn a phrase so that it will set up a poem's meaning out of a seemingly banal course of observations or set the hook of our interest in a poem. The following is from *Spring Pools* (Frost, *The Complete Poems of Robert Frost,* 1965):

> *The trees that have it in their pent-up buds*
> *To darken nature and be summer woods—*
> *Let them think twice before they use their powers*
> *To blot out and drink up and sweep away*
> *These flowery waters and these watery flowers*
> *From snow that melted only yesterday.*

The line "Let them think twice before they use their powers" begins to form or set an attitude about a simple observation of nature. We hear a hook in the first line of Frost's poem *Mending Wall:* "Something there is that doesn't love a wall … ." We hear this line and instantly feel the discomfort. Like hearing a minor chord, we yearn for some resolution. "What?" we ask. "What doesn't love a wall? Why love a wall? Why not love a wall?" I try to create a similar effect with my father's adage at the beginning of my anecdotal story, "Good Bob, Bad Bob": "Growing up, I remember hearing my father say, 'The reason why it says in the Bible to love they neighbor is because it's such a damn hard thing to do.'"

Of course, poetry is not the only model of beautiful nature writing. Writers such as Ernest Hemingway, Ralph W. Emerson and Barry Lopez have been inspirational. You may have some of your own favorites. The particular advantage to poetry is that it is often written with an attention to sound and rhythm. A good way to educate yourself about the musical qualities of language is to go to poetry festivals or literary readings.

Becoming Salmon. Often the teller's body begins to move in a rhythm that is the living rhythm or movement of the subject (salmon leaping out from an enclosure into a river). Timing is exactly as it is in life.

Photos courtesy Diane Kulpinski

A job will force us to make a change that we wouldn't make of our own volition or will. During my fifth year of storytelling, I had become increasingly annoyed by dramatics in storytelling. My impression was that the general public believed that what made storytelling interesting was the dramatics (sound effects, gestures, props, costumes and so on). Whereas I felt there was something more subtle that gave storytelling its true power. Be careful what you ask for! About this time, I was invited to work with a Klezmer band (Eastern European Jewish folk music) on a grant to produce a program on the Hassidic music and storytelling tradition. Hassidic tales, as previously described in chapter 1, evolved out of a mystical sect of Judaism in which the stories are told anecdotally, when "called for" or needed and often only to an audience of one. In order to maintain this intimate quality, in sometimes large performance venues, I sat on a high stool, used a single microphone and essentially tied my hands. The only media left to me was the story, word choice and voice. This situation sharpened my attention to variations of speed and rhythms within the composition, sounds of words and use of silence along with the other musical qualities referred to in chapter 3. In effect, I was kind of like a singer in the band. I became more attuned to how two different tellings might be almost identical and yet one will have a greater quality of lightness. Like a musician, I began to feel the story as a whole composition—that a piece moves forward in response to the audience's need. Sometimes this feeling moves the story (or parts thereof) faster and sometimes slower. In the course of this telling, a teller discovers un-premeditated speaking rhythms. The experience feels like you are in harmony with a horse's gait at high canter, riding on instinct and nothing is predictable.

GESTURE AND MOVEMENT

I discovered masks from the Natives of the Northwest coast while I was working as a teacher at a science museum. These masks are often made with the same materials and colors. Yet with a distinct change in line or shape they create an archetype of a particular animal or character. Cannibal Woman, for example, is always portrayed with a large, open, O-shaped mouth. She is the archetype of swallowing or our fear of death. When I discovered the story of *At'At' Hila Monster Woman at the Coast* (Wasco, Oregon) in an anthropological text—a story in which she sends her victims to their death by tying them to a cradle board, throwing them out into the ocean and calling "Go forever!"—I had the idea to speak the O in "go" in a long, hallow, eerie manner. I let my face (especially the mouth) become for those moments the same Cannibal Woman I saw in the masks. The masks became an inspiration for both voice and gesture.

Actually, the mask idea went through an evolution. Shortly before I discovered Northwest coastal Native masks, I was teaching my first summer program with a traveling outdoor school, the High Country School. I had just discovered Coyote and would become Coyote whenever I wanted to tease the students into a desired behavior. They couldn't help but fall prey to the fun and often demanded the reappearance of the trickster at other times. "Make that Coyote face, again!" they would say. Finally, it dawned on me that something was appearing in my facial expression and gesture that was consistently recognizable as this character. With exposure to the Northwest coastal masks in my work at the science museum the following fall, I began to create characters with intentional body and masklike facial gestures. After a few years, I lost interest in the idea of intentionally created gestures because I felt that my audiences were delighting in the characterizations and the dramatics, and not necessarily remembering the stories. Also, the characterizations began to feel very canned.

The next stage of development gave me great delight. I worked at feeling the characters, deeply in my body and voice, before I became them. I let the mask or body gesture change based on how I felt or saw the character at a particular moment in the story. This gave rise to totally fresh characterizations that sprang up in new places in the story and imbued the story with an authenticity—a living quality—that seemed to break down some kind of wall between myself and the audience and allowed both of us to sink deeper into the story world. This stage of evolution came about the same time I decided to develop my feeling senses by observing wildlife wherever I could.

Photos courtesy Diane Kulpinski

Full body fall. Some experiences in the story call for a full body gesture. Experiment and develop some consciousness about large gestures. Sometimes, too many large gestures or too large of a gesture distracts the audience from the story. Even a long fall can be created with a small gesture.

133

Becoming Coyote. Notice the subtle transformations that occur in head position, mouth, teeth and hands while the teller is seeing and feeling the Coyote character she wants to become.

Photos courtesy Diane Kulpinski

Working with wildlife at the Audubon Rehabilitation Center in Portland, Oregon, helped me develop a character voice for the dove in "The Hundredth Dove" (*The Bird's Tale*, 1985) and an appreciation for crows that led to the later development of my anecdotal story, "The Crow's Story" (*Coyote Gets a Cadillac*

and Other Eye-Opening Earth Tales, 1991). Wildlife viewing has been invaluable for development of animal gestures and movement. Although I have never seen wolves in the wild, many long hours of sitting in enclosures with captive wolves provided some essence of their movement and spirit, which helped me bring them alive again in *Wolf Stories: Myths and True Life Tales from Around the World* (1993). Some artists are able to portray a subject without spending hours observing the subject, but I am not one of them. I prefer to let the fine details of a subject permeate my being. Although I feel confident re-creating an atmosphere of Russia in a Russian fairy tale (even thought I have never been in Russia), I would not feel comfortable attempting to re-create an animal or aspect of nature without full immersion. Perhaps this is because I value nature so much and want all of her aspects to breathe true to life and true to their archetype within my storytelling.

An art museum, the National Gallery of Art in Washington, D.C., invited me to develop a performance of Greek myths that had been the inspiration of several paintings in their permanent collection. In this project, I brought together my understanding of poetics with an expanded understanding of archetype and archetypal movement to create the largeness and power of these classic stories. In order to develop an understanding for the archetypes in the myths (primarily expressed as gods and goddesses), I studied not only the specific paintings in the permanent collection, but also other paintings and sculptures of these gods and goddesses at the National Gallery and at other art museums. I never took a specific gesture or movement from these depictions, but I filled myself up with all of the ways artists defined these archetypes through the centuries.

Two other sources of inspiration aided this process during this time period: (1) background research, and (2) personal dreams. I had been reading several books on the ideas of Carl G. Jung, the famous Swiss psychologist who could be considered the father of archetypal psychology. I had also had a powerful dream involving one of the archetypes I had been pursuing. The dream imagery was striking in its visual vitality, color and my strong bodily memory of the experience. It was striking also because I found the same imagery exactly described and explained a week after I had the dream in one of the research books I was reading.

From these and many other impressions, I created my own mental images of the archetypes. Then, from these images coupled with a feeling of an archetype's essence, I found original movements and gestures.

Usefulness of Classes and Workshops

Of course, classes and workshops can be helpful, but what kinds and what should you expect from them? I have always found life itself more inspirational to my artistic development than most classes, although I have found a few good ones. Since story is a mirror of life, it is important not to look to classes and workshops to give you a prescription for how to tell a story. Rather, search for your inspiration from interdisciplinary sources as described earlier in this chapter and try classes, say, in the visual arts, poetry or music. Remember Ansel Adams' statement about how much the cello taught him about photography, and, after all, storytelling *is* a three-part art.

I always found it very ironic that over the years people have frequently commented that I moved like a dancer and must have had lots of dance training. For the first fifteen years of my storytelling career, I had not taken one dance class (with the exception of periodic aerobics classes in which I noticed, once, how winglike my arms could be). In two different attempts at dance class as a child, I always felt like I had two left feet. Perhaps the reason why I move like a dancer in my storytelling is because within the story, I create the music and the tempo. I believe that complete immersion in the imagery of the story—an immersion in which all of the senses are awake and contributing to the creation of the imagery—is how to find authentic movement and gesture. This is not to say that mirrors are not helpful, but they can take one's focus away from this internal image-making process.

Recently, I began working with a dancer, Vincent Martinez, in a performance on landscape entitled *Visible Distance*. Since I have had a love of landscape painting since I was a child, I wanted to create a storytelling performance in which gesture and movement were larger and more visual than I could make as an individual (diverging far from the style of the Hassidic tales). In our work together, I became interested in taking workshops from Vincent and invited him to teach movement during a one-week workshop on storytelling in natural history interpretation, which I give with my colleague, Linda Sussman. Vincent's way of working with movement is completely grounded in this same concept of total immersion in the imagination. Nothing is taught in a recipe, "this is how it is done" style. All of his teaching is a process of exploration based on developing internal images. For example, in one of his activities, which he calls Coyote dancing, he asks the participants to form a large circle. The music begins, and at their own whim they can enter the circle and dance. Inside the circle, they must dance as Coyote, always backward and doing whatever is wild, unpredictable and unconventional. They must become a heyoke. When participants are tired, they can retreat to themselves at the edge of the circle and watch the other Coyotes until they feel drawn in again. The image here is not as specific as becoming a Coyote, but rather becoming the archetype of the Coyote, heyoke, trickster or wild one. Perhaps a participant would find a movement in this activity that could be used to express any wild being.

Out of a workshop of these kind of activities you might find only one movement to use in a story, but your general attention to how you move and don't move will be heightened. In addition, your imaginative thinking will be stimulated, which, in turn, may stimulate other ideas regarding story structure, how a character should speak and so on. Even when I don't have an opportunity to take a workshop, I do some type of physical activity, such as running, just to stimulate my attention to movement. During the development of my wolf myths, for example, I imagined myself as a wolf trotting while I was out for a run. The point is to find opportunities to move while imagining the telling of the story. This stimulates the collaboration: The body gives the mind ideas and the mind gives the body ideas. This same process can work for voice. As mentioned in chapter 9, singing a story is a good way to develop your attention to word sounds or sentence rhythms.

A workshop worth taking often attempts to teach one art form through imaginative activities involving other art forms. The best workshop on voice I ever took was with Richard Armstrong from the Roy Hart Theater (described in chapter 3). He used body movement and imaginative situations to help participants find qualities of voice they never thought they could make. Practitioners of the martial arts know this relationship which voice has to body movement, as certain vocalizations are believed to be integral to the power of a strike movement.

Eurythmy is an art form that has been especially inspirational to me. It is not well known in the United States but can be observed in most Waldorf Schools. Eurythmy is not dance. It is, among other things, a way of gesturing sound—a kind of visual speech. When I practice eurythmy, I develop a deeper feeling for the moods an individual sound can create. This, in turn, awakens my ear for sound and word choice. Some of these mood/sound relationships were described in chapter 3 and were partially inspired by eurythmy training. The main school for eurythmy in the United States is located in Chestnut Ridge, New York, but brief exposure can be found in Waldorf teacher training programs around the United States (see appendix).

In closing, I would like to reinforce the idea that, for me, life itself is the best source of inspiration for finding voice and movement. Here is a story about one such source and how to use silence for dramatic effect:

> I was driving slowly down an irrigation ditch, a dirt road that makes a shortcut between my house and that of a friend. Up ahead, a truck was parked in the way. It belonged to Heavy, an elderly neighbor who was originally from Minnesota and from a time when conversation was an art. He was repairing another neighbor's fence, but stopped when he saw me coming and moved his truck so I could get by. Then, he sauntered over to the rider's side window for a word or two. I reached over and rolled down the window.
>
> "Hey, Heavy," I said, "hope yer not workin' too hard."
> "Yep, yep—well it's a beautiful day—isn't it?" he said.
> "Yeah," I said. "It is! A very beautiful day!"
> "Yep, it's a good day for mending fences." (silence, silence, silence)
> "But then it's a good day for goin' fishin', too."

Our teachers are everywhere.

Epilogue

PASSIONATE FACTS:
TAKING THE LISTENER BEYOND INFORMATION

Ask any scientist or historian to share a fact about which they are passionate and listen as a great story unfolds. That which we call fact is merely the title page for an entire saga. To tell nature's story or the story of human culture, we as interpreters need to see the story that is sleeping among these scattered bones we call facts. Stories of all kinds are constantly happening all around us—in our dreams, in the news, in history books, in the mountains that break above the horizon line and in the soil below our feet. Yet, in our work as scholars, interpreters or educators, we feel pressed to give information, and often we surrender to a way of describing this dynamic living world that has the one-dimensional quality I call "information speak." This way of giving content relies on a narrow, if not monotone, use of voice, categorization as a way to show difference, numbered measurement as the only way to create imagery and definitions that are isolated from their context.

By contrast, we must search for a way to give the same content as story. By story, I don't mean necessarily the grand opera of myth performance. I mean simply to speak in a manner that lets a subject breathe, show its color and character—in short, lets it live and shows its relevance to life. Story speaking transforms the one-dimensional quality of "information speak" by simply broadening the ways in which something may be shown (translates information into imagery) and by creating a sense of journey (shows relationship and context). With these two qualities, information becomes experience and all of our senses—sight, feeling, taste, touch and smell—are engaged.

These qualities give story its powerful influence on the human memory. If the imagery and the relationships revealed in the story's journey are engaging, then the messages of the story will be carried by the listener, like a seed in fertile soil, beyond the moment of initial entertainment. Therefore, the interpreter/educator must constantly inquire: What makes a story engaging? We must put aside our fascination with the material trappings of interpretation and remember:

The story's the thing. Story is the heart and soul of every effective slide show, film, puppet show, living history or costumed character presentation. Initially, children may be very impressed by a larger-than-life Mickey Mouse, but, the interpreter should ask, did the mouse share any episode from its mouse life? The puppets may be colorful, slapstick or sing a catchy tune in the hippest musical style, but was the audience engaged by them as characters with experiences and travails worth listening to?

The symbolic stories (myths, fairy tales, religious) from every culture give us various models of the human experience and natural phenomenon in story speak. One of the best ways to develop your sense of story is to study these symbolic stories and their archetypes. Often, the archetypal presentation of a natural subject in world mythology can give clues for how best to tell this same subject's scientific story. For instance, the most ancient wolf myths reveal positive aspects of the wolf that have surfaced again, after centuries of misunderstanding, in recent scientific research and new public admiration. Once you become familiar with archetypes, you will begin to see them in your own dreams, in scientific facts, in histories and in the occurrences of your daily life (anecdotes). The boundaries between the concrete and the metaphorical will begin to fade.

Become familiar with all kinds of stories and the way in which all of the artistic disciplines tell stories. Then, begin with your own anecdotes. Your own experiences are stories so close to you that you may hardly recognize them as stories—and because of this, they will feel easier for you to tell than more elaborate story forms. All biological observations can be told either as personal anecdote or as scientific observation. The difference is only in the telling. There is an intimacy about personal anecdote that allows it to come up in conversation with the public in a spontaneous, seemingly un-premeditated, style. In the casual atmosphere of walking between exhibits or meeting along a wilderness trail, the public is less guarded and the anecdote has a potential for great effectiveness.

Let your telling of anecdotes lead you into the telling of the other great stories: histories, natural histories, legends, folktales, fairy tales, myths and dreams. Seek to find ways to weave or couple these different types of stories together in a presentation. As a result, they may mirror or reinforce each other. In effect, your interpretive themes will emerge magically between the stories, synergistically. Likewise, "framing" a speech or interpretive talk with a story is very powerful. The images of the opening story can be called up again and again through the course of the speech, reinforcing major themes and concepts.

Story speaking is a dance, whereas information speaking is a kind of attack. In the process of learning this dance, you need to practice the art of listening, self-listening and self-witnessing. Listening, a dying art in many parts of modern society, should be a priority in our personal as well as public educational efforts. With awakened listening, everything around you becomes a potential inspiration for a story or the expression of that story in movement, voice or a character's words. Self-listening or self-witnessing guards against a self-righteous tone of voice and a pedantic attitude. Also, it helps one maintain a sense of humor and ability to laugh at one's self. Self-witnessing helps you to see and hear all of the things that go on during your presentation (often distractions) and have the presence of mind to incorporate them, spontaneously. Often, the incorporation of distractions can augment the meaning of your story or presentation and create relationship between you and your audience and between both of you and your immediate environment. I remember telling the old English folktale, "The Hundredth Dove," in an outdoor setting when a white dove flew into the stage area at a perfect moment in the story.

Do your research. Know your subject: Know its scientific or historic story and its mythology. Study and question your audiences' and your own responses to this knowledge. Then speak out of your love for the subject and its story. Don't lose sight of your passion for the story (or if you do, develop an interest in why). Let formulas, rules or advice regarding storytelling presentations inform, inspire or challenge you, but not dull your pursuit of a passionate engagement with the story. Become interested in the arts. How does art differ from entertainment or education? What does it mean to be an artist? What does it mean that each one of us has the capacity to be an artist? Think of yourself as an artist more than as an interpreter or educator. Remember Coyote—hero, creator and fool of Native American mythology. In the image of creator, Coyote was never satisfied within the bounds of accepted practices—curious, questioning, sniffing around in unknown territory—vulnerable, falls to his death and is reborn. "So, as Coyote imagined it," they say, "so, it was created! Sometimes Coyote brought back good things and changed the way society thought and did things."

Appendix

Related Organizations

National Association for the Preservation and Perpetuation of Storytelling (NAPPS)
P.O. Box 309
Jonesborough, TN 37659
(615) 753-2171

National Association of Interpreters (NAI)
P.O. Box 1892
Fort Collins, CO 80522
(303) 491-6434

NAI Sections:

Council for American Indian Interpretation (CAII)

Resource Interpretation Heritage Tourism (RIHT)

Zoo/Wildlife Park/Aquarium

Nature Center Directors and Administrators

National Science Teachers Association
1742 Connecticut Ave., NW
Washington, D.C. 20009-1171

North American Association of Environmental Educators
P.O. Box 400
Troy, OH 45373

Schools and Workshops

The Passionate Fact: Storytelling Residency for Science and Cultural Interpretation
with Susan Strauss and Linda Sussman, Ph.D.
March in Bend, Oregon
fall and summer at University of Idaho, Moscow, Idaho
contact:
Susan Strauss
P.O. Box 1141
Bend, OR 97709
(503) 382-2888

Living Stories: A Training in Storytelling
with Linda Sussman
fall and spring
contact:
Linda Sussman
4747 SW Hamilton St.
Portland, OR 97221
(503) 226-3893

Laura Simms' Storytelling Residency
summer
contact:
Laura Simms
814 Broadway
New York, NY 10003
(212) 674-3479

Eurythmy Association of North America
84 Suffolk La.
Garden City, NY 11530
contact:
Leonore Russell
(516) 741-7167

School of Eurythmy
285 Hungry Hollow Rd.
Chestnut Ridge, NY 10977
contact:
Dorothea Mier
(914) 352-5020

Vincent Martinez
contact:
Body Moves Studio
918 SW Yamhill
Portland, OR 97205
(503) 227-3578

Bibliography

Abbey, Edward. *Desert Solitaire: A Season in the Wilderness.* New York: Simon and Schuster, 1968.

Afanas'ev, Aleksandr. *Russian Fairy Tales.* New York: Pantheon Books, 1945.

Anderson, Jim. *Tales from a Northwest Naturalist.* Caldwell, Idaho: Caxton Printers, 1992.

Bierhorst, John. *The Mythology of Mexico and Central America.* New York: W. Morrow, 1990.

———. *The Mythology of North America.* New York: W. Morrow, 1985.

———. *The Mythology of South America.* New York: W. Morrow, 1988.

Blue Cloud, Peter. *Elderberry Flute Song: Contemporary Coyote Tales.* Trumansburg, N.Y.: Crossing Press, 1982.

Bly, Robert. *News of the Universe.* San Francisco: Sierra Club Books, 1980.

———. *What Have I Ever Lost by Dying? Collected Prose Poems.* New York: Harper-Collins, 1992.

Boer, Charles. *The Homeric Hymns.* Chicago: Swallow Press, 1970.

Burke, James. *Connections.* Boston: Little, Brown, 1978.

Caduto, Michael J., and Joseph Bruchac. *Keepers of the Earth: Native American Stories and Environmental Activities for Children.* Golden, Colo.: Fulcrum Publishing, 1988. (For other books in the series, contact Fulcrum Publishing.)

Callahan, Bob. *A Jaime De Angulo Reader.* Berkeley, Calif.: Turtle Island, 1979.

Cameron, Anne. *Daughters of Copper Woman.* Vancouver, B.C.: Press Gang Publishers, 1981.

Campbell, Joseph. *The Hero with a Thousand Faces.* Cleveland and New York: Meridian Books, 1956.

———. *Occidental Mythology: The Masks of God.* New York: Viking Penguin Group, 1964.

Carrey, Conley Barton. *Snake River of Hells Canyon.* Cambridge, Idaho: Backeddy Books, 1979.

Chief Seattle. *Aboriginal American Oratory.* N.p., n.d.

Cornell, Joseph. *Sharing Nature with Children*. Nevada City, Calif.: Ananda Publications, 1979.

Cushing, Frank Hamilton. *Zuni Folk Tales*. Tucson: University of Arizona Press, 1986.

Dooling, D. M. *Parabola Magazine*. New York: Society for the Study of Myth and Tradition, quarterly.

Edsman, Carl-Martin. "The Story of the Bear Wife in Nordic Tradition." Stockholm: Ethnos 1–2, 1956.

Erdoes, Richard. *The Sound of Flutes and Other Indian Legends*. New York: Pantheon Books, 1976.

Frost, Robert. *The Complete Poems of Robert Frost*. New York: Holt, Rinehart and Winston, 1965.

Grimm Brothers. *The Complete Grimm's Fairy Tales*. New York: Pantheon Books, 1944.

Haines, Aubrey L. *The Yellowstone Story*. Yellowstone National Park, Wyo.: Yellowstone Library and Museum Association (with Colorado Associated University Press), 1977.

Hartzell, Hal Jr. *The Yew Tree: A Thousand Whispers*. Eugene, Oreg.: Hulogosi, 1991.

Haslam, Gerald. *Western Writing*. Albuquerque: University of New Mexico Press, 1974.

Hemingway, Ernest. *Collected Stories*. New York: Collier Books, 1966.

Holland, Kevin Crossley. *The Norse Myths*. New York: Pantheon Books, 1980.

Innes, Mary M. *The Metamorphoses of Ovid*. New York: Penguin Books, 1955.

Josephy, Alvin M. Jr. *The Nez Perce Indians and the Opening of the Northwest*. Lincoln and London: University of Nebraska Press, 1966.

Kittredge, William. *Hole in the Sky*. N.p.: David McKay, 1992.

Kroeber, Alfred. *Karok Myths*. Berkeley, Los Angeles and London: University of California Press, 1980.

———. *Yurok Myths*. Berkeley, Los Angeles and London: University of California Press, 1976.

Kroeber, Karl. *Traditional Literatures of the American Indian: Texts and Interpretations*. Lincoln and London: University of Nebraska Press, 1981.

Lao-tzu. *Tao Te Ching*. Middlesex, England: Penguin Books, 1963.

Lawlor, Robert. *Sacred Geometry: Philosophy and Practice*. London: Thames and Hudson, 1982.

Leopold, Aldo. *A Sand County Almanac*. New York: Tamarac Press, 1977.

Levin, Meyer. *Classic Hassidic Tales*. New York: Penguin Books, 1932.

Lopez, Barry. *Desert Notes: Reflections in the Eye of a Raven*. Kansas City, Miss.: Sheed, Andrews and McMeel, 1976.

———. *Giving Birth to Thunder, Sleeping with His Daughter: Coyote Builds North America*. Kansas City, Miss.: Sheed, Andrews and McMeel, 1977.

———. *Of Wolves and Men*. New York: Charles Scribner's Sons, 1978.

Lovelock, J. E. *Gaia: A New Look at Life on Earth*. Oxford: Oxford University Press, 1979.

MacKenzie, Donald A. *Teutonic Myth and Legend*. New York: William H. Wise, 1934.

Malotki, Ekkehart, and Michael Lomatuway'ma. *Hopi Coyote Tales*. Lincoln and London: University of Nebraska Press, 1984.

Margolin, Malcolm. *The Way We Lived: California Indian Reminiscences, Stories and Songs*. Berkeley, Calif.: Heyday Books, 1981.

Marriott, Alice, and Carol K. Rachlin. *American Indian Mythology*. New York: New American Library, 1972.

Mech, David L. *The Way of the Wolf*. Stillwater, Minn.: Voyageur Press, 1991.

Melville, Jacobs. *Coos Myth Texts*. Seattle: University of Washington, 1940.

Moyne, John, and Coleman Barks, eds. *Open Secret*. Putney, Vt.: Threshold Books, 1984.

Nash, Roderick. *The American Environment: Readings in the History of Conservation*. Reading, Mass.: Addison-Wesley, 1968.

Neihardt, John G. *Black Elk Speaks: Being the Life Story of a Holy Man of the Oglala Sioux*. New York: Simon and Schuster, 1972.

Norman, Howard. *Northern Tales: Traditional Stories of Eskimo and Indian Peoples*. New York: Pantheon Books, 1990.

———. *The Wishing Bone Cycle: Narrative Poems from the Swampy Cree Indians*. New York: Stonehill Publishing, 1976.

Norse, Elliott A. *Ancient Forests of the Pacific Northwest*. Washington, D.C.: Island Press/Wilderness Society, 1990.

O'Callahan, Jay. *Herman and Margaret* (cassette). Marshfield, Mass.: self-published, n.d., ph: 617-837-0962.

Oliver, Mary. *New and Selected Poems by Mary Oliver*. Boston: Beacon Press, 1992.

Phinney, Archie. *Nez Perce Texts*. New York: Columbia University Press, 1936.

Radin, Paul. *The Trickster, A Study in American Indian Mythology*. New York: Schocken Books, 1972.

Ramsey, Jarold. *Coyote Was Going There: Indian Literature of the Oregon Country*. Seattle and London: University of Washington Press, 1977.

Reid, Bill, and Robert Bringhurst. *The Raven Steals the Light*. Seattle: University of Washington Press, 1984.

Roessel, Robert A. Jr. *Coyote Stories of the Navaho People*. Chinle, Ariz.: Dine, 1968.

Rothenberg, Jerome. *Shaking the Pumpkin: Traditional Poetry of the Indian North Americas*. New York: Doubleday, 1972.

Ryden, Hope. *God's Dog: The North American Coyote*. New York: Lyons and Burford, 1975.

Sapir, Edward. *Wishram Texts*. New York: AMS Press, 1974.

Schultz, James W. *Why Gone Those Times: Blackfoot Tales*. Norman: University of Oklahoma Press, 1974.

Schwenk, Theodor. *Sensitive Chaos: The Creation of Flowing Forms in Water and Air*. London: Rudolf Steiner Press, 1965.

Shah, Idries. *The Exploits of the Incomparable Mulla Nasrudin*. London: Octagon Press, 1983.

————. *The Pleasantries of the Incredible Mulla Nasrudin.* London: Octagon Press, 1983.

Stone, Merlin. *Ancient Mirrors of Womanhood: A Treasury of Goddess and Heroine Lore from Around the World.* Boston: Beacon Press, 1979.

Strauss, Susan. *And for Kids.* Bend, Oreg.: Strauss, 1990. Audiotape.

————. *The Bird's Tale.* Bend, Oreg.: Strauss, 1985. Audiotape.

————. *Coyote Gets a Cadillac and Other Eye-Opening Earth Tales.* Bend, Oreg.: Strauss, 1991. Audiotape.

————. *Coyote Stories for Children: Tales from Native America.* Hillsboro, Oreg.: Beyond Words, 1991.

————. *Oh! That Coyote: Native American Coyote Tales for Reading Aloud.* Bend, Oreg.: Strauss, 1983.

————. *Tracks, Tracks, Tracks.* Bend, Oreg.: Strauss, 1985.

————. *Witches, Queens and Goddesses: Mythic Images of the Feminine.* Bend, Oreg.: Strauss, 1987. Audiotape.

————. *Wolf Stories: Myths and True Life Tales from Around the World.* Hillsboro, Oreg.: Beyond Words, 1993.

————. *Yiddish and Hassidic Tales of Wonder.* Bend, Oreg.: Strauss, 1988. Audiotape.

Swann, Brian. *Smoothing the Ground: Essays on Native American Oral Literature.* Berkeley, Los Angeles and London: University of California Press, 1983.

Swanton, John. "Haida Texts and Myths." *Bureau of American Ethnology,* Bul. 29.

Tedlock, Dennis. *Popol Vuh: The Definitive Edition of the Mayan Book of the Dawn of Life and the Glories of Gods and Kings.* New York: Simon and Schuster, 1985.

Thomas, Dylan. *The Collected Stories.* New York: New Direction, 1938.

Thompson, Stith. *Tales of the North American Indians.* Bloomington: Indiana University Press, 1958.

Trimble, Stephen. *Words from the Land.* Salt Lake City: Biggs-Smith, 1989.

Uchida, Yoshiko. *The Magic Listening Cap: More Folk Tales from Japan.* Berkeley: Creative Arts Book Company, 1987.

Walker, Barbara K. *A Treasury of Turkish Folktales.* Hamden, Conn.: Linnet Books, 1988.

Westervelt, W. D. *Hawaiian Legends of Volcanoes.* Tokyo: C. E. Tuttle, 1963.

Williams, Strephon K. *The Jungian-Senoi Dreamwork Manual.* Berkeley: Journey Press, 1985.

Index

Story structure, 6, 24–26, 29–32, 80, 84, 117, 126
Symbol, 6, 15, 16, 22, 42, 46, 54–57, 62, 63, 66, 88, 103, 113, 140

T

Tape recorder, 121, 122
Television, 1, 3, 7, 10, 38, 70, 103
Tempo, 24, 40
Theme, 9
Thoreau, Henry David, 1
Tilden, Freeman, 4, 24
Time, sanctified, 90, 103–105
Timing, 131
Tragedy, 14, 49, 50
Trees, 6, 19, 22, 23, 32, 56–59, 67, 71, 72, 79–82, 85, 87, 93, 94, 98, 100, 115–119, 121, 129
Trickster, 50–52, 97, 99, 137
Truth, 3, 4, 6, 13–15, 20–23, 44, 46, 52–56, 61, 68, 80, 82, 93, 94, 97, 99, 106, 108, 112, 114

V

Values, 14, 16, 44, 46, 49, 55, 76
Violence, 102, 103
Voice, 3, 4, 8, 24, 25, 29, 32, 35, 41–43, 46, 50, 83, 127, 129, 132, 135, 138, 141
Volcanic, 64, 65, 85

W

Waldorf Schools, 76
Water, 19, 65, 77, 78, 85, 86, 97–99, 101, 116–119, 124, 125
Weed archetype, 79, 80, 93
Wolves, 8, 20, 23, 28, 29, 34, 38, 59–61, 63, 73, 74, 114, 136, 138, 140
Workshops, 136–138, 142, 143
Worm, 85

Y

Yarns, 8, 14

Z

Zarathustra, 68